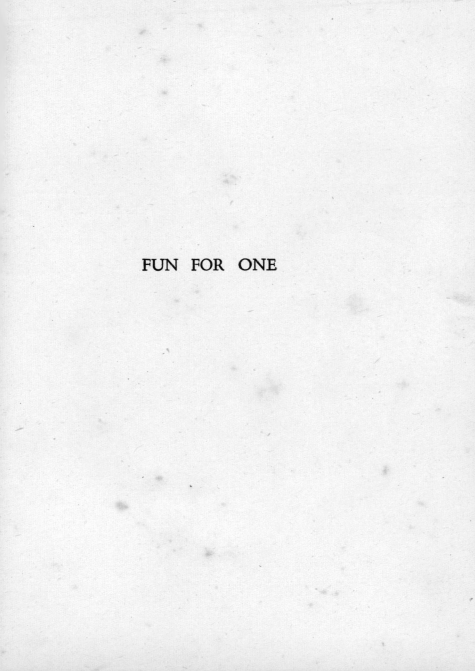

FUN FOR ONE

FUN FOR ONE

EDITED BY

E. M. GOODRICK

THOMAS NELSON & SONS LTD

LONDON EDINBURGH PARIS MELBOURNE
TORONTO AND NEW YORK

First published, 1943

CONTENTS

PART I: INDOORS

PART II: YOUR PETS

CONTENTS

PART III: OUT OF DOORS

PART I
INDOORS

FUN FOR ONE

GAMES TO PLAY BY YOURSELF

MOST games start with the instructions, "Divide the players into teams," but here are some games that you can enjoy by yourself.

MARBLE ARCH

Find a piece of stiff card about twelve inches long and cut five inch-and-a-half-high arches in it. Number each arch. Bend the ends of the card round so that it will stand upright on the table or ground.

From a distance of about three feet roll marbles through the arches, scoring according to the numbers. Increase the distance as your skill grows.

LONG WORDS AND LITTLE WORDS

This is a pencil-and-paper game for a wet day. Think of a long word (or find one in the dictionary) and write it at the top of your paper. Then see how many smaller words you can make from it. Set yourself rules, such as making words of not less than three letters and using the same letter twice in one word only if it appears twice in the big word, and so on.

PLEASE TO REMEMBER

Get together a fairly large number of odds and ends and place them on the table. Study them for two minutes, trying to fix each item in your memory.

At the end of the two minutes cover the things over and make a list of as many as you can remember.

TAPE-MEASURE MARATHON

You can play this game with two or more tiddly-winks of different colours, racing them against each other.

Stretch out a tape-measure on the floor or table and put a weight at each end to prevent it curling up. Then invent hazards or advantages, such as " Wait for a six," " Move to 3 inches," " Go back to the beginning." Write these on slips of paper and place them at intervals under the tape-measure. If you prefer it you can write the hazards in a list, " 2 inches—Wait for a six," " 5 inches—Move to 3 inches," and so forth, and refer to the list after each throw.

The tiddlywinks have to get from one end of the tape to the other, obeying the instructions they meet on the way. Their progress is, of course, determined by the throw of the dice.

THE DOTTED SQUARE

Mark out on paper a square of eight rows with eight circles in each row, as shown here.

O O O O O O O O
O O O O O O O O
O O O O O O O O
O O O O O O O O
O O O O O O O O
O O O O O O O O
O O O O O O O O
O O O O O O O O

Then shut your eyes and with a pencil make a mark on the paper. Blacken out the circle nearest to the pencil mark, then proceed to blacken seven more circles. Each one that you blacken must be the only one blackened in its line, counting the line in all directions, horizontally, vertically, and diagonally.

It may seem difficult at first, but on whatever circle you begin it is possible to add the other seven blackings. Suppose, for instance, you landed on the third circle of the fifth horizontal line. Then the puzzle could be completed thus :

1st horizontal row, black the 5th circle.
2nd   ,,   ,,   ,,   8th ,,
3rd   ,,   ,,   ,,   4th ,,
4th   ,,   ,,   ,,   1st ,,
5th   ,,   ,,   ,,   3rd ,,
6th   ,,   ,,   ,,   6th ,,
7th   ,,   ,,   ,,   2nd ,,
8th   ,,   ,,   ,,   7th ,,

MAKE-BELIEVE ZOO

Make a point of cutting out pictures of funny animals or people whenever you come across them. First cut round the whole outline, then cut off the heads and put them in one box or envelope, the bodies in another, and the legs in a third.

When you are ready to play with them, bring out the boxes and pick heads, bodies, and legs at random, putting them together to make complete animals. You will find that most of your concoctions are queerer than anything ever seen at the Zoo !

HOLIDAY JIGSAWS

A rather similar pastime to Make-believe Zoo is to look out all those carefully hoarded picture post cards, sent by holiday-making friends, and cut each into wiggly sections. Of course, you must keep the sections of each post card in a separate envelope, or they will become hopelessly mixed.

When you are in the mood, bring out these home-made jigsaws and while away some enthralling minutes by putting them together.

TOWNS AND RIVERS

Here's a writing game that will test your general knowledge ! Take a sheet of paper and on the left-hand side of it write the following list : Country, River, Town, Girl's name, Boy's name, Animal, Bird, Tree, Flower, Fruit. Then, beginning with A and working right through the alphabet, make lists alongside of a country, a river, etc., all starting with the same letter.

For instance, your first list, starting with A, might be : America, Avon, Axminster, Alice, Alfred, Ape, Albatross, Ash, Aster, Apple.

DARTS—REAL AND SUBSTITUTE

If you are allowed to use the family dartboard you can always be sure of some fun. If not, make a dartboard with which you can do no damage, by

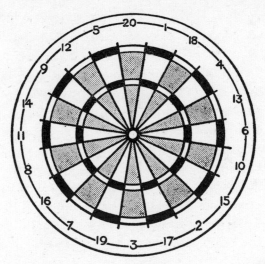

drawing one on card and marking it off into twenty sections, with two concentric circles in the middle. The outer of these circles counts as 25, and the inner—or bullseye—as 50. If you place this board flat at one end of the table your " darts " can be three tiddleywinks or paper pellets flicked on to it, or propelled with the aid of a rubber band, this latter method being the more exciting !

Round the Clock is played by aiming at each number in turn, starting at 1, ending at 20, and finishing off with 25 to be followed by a bullseye. You are allowed only three shots at each number and, once your dart has gone home, there is no need to try again. If, after three tries, you have still failed, you score against yourself the number which you have failed to hit. The game, when you are playing by yourself, is to see how quickly you can get round the clock.

Cricket is a well-known darts game which really needs two teams of people, but you can adapt it for one player quite easily. First, toss a coin to see if you will bat or bowl first. Heads you bat, tails you bowl. If you bowl, give yourself a quarter of an hour in which to take 10 wickets. This means 10 bullseyes. At the end of that time make a note of the number of wickets you have managed to take, then go in to bat.

When batting, your darts may go anywhere on the board—except on the bullseye. If it should land there it scores a wicket instead of a run. As in ordinary darts, a hit in the outer ring of the board doubles the score, and one in the half-way ring means a triple score for that section.

At the end of another quarter of an hour add up your runs and set them against your wickets, *e.g.* 176 for 8. Then (after a refreshment interval !) put your " other side " in, which means that you will begin all over again and try to beat your earlier effort.

SOME STUNTS TO PRACTISE

NOW for some stunts, which are great fun to try by yourself and are useful at a party. Your friends will long to tie themselves up in similar knots!

TOEING THE MATCHBOX

Stand with both feet together then place an empty matchbox on the floor beside the little toe of your right foot.

Next, pass your right hand round the inner side of your right knee and over your right instep to pick up the box. You may bend your knees, but you must not touch the floor with your left hand for support.

PUSH AND PICK-UP

You will need a matchbox again for this. Hold it in one hand and toe a line on the floor—the edge of a rug or a particular spot in the lino pattern will do.

Now, place your free hand on the nape of your neck, sit on your heels, put your matchbox hand behind you and between your ankles, and place the box on the floor as far in front of you as possible. Now stand upright again.

Then, placing one hand on your neck as before, repeat the performance and pick the box up.

BOX BITING

A useful toy is the matchbox, so here is another stunt to try with it.

Stand the box on the toe of one foot and try to pick it up in your teeth. You must not touch the floor with your hands, but—as a special concession— you may bend your knees.

The best way is to grip the ankle of the box-bearing foot with both hands, while you raise the free foot behind you to keep the balance.

THE FLOATING ARM

As a change from matchboxes, try this experiment. Stand with one side to the wall, a few inches from it. Press the back of your hand steadily against the wall for a minute, then stand away with that arm relaxed. In a very short time your arm will begin to float upwards of its own accord.

PUZZLES AND POSERS

HERE are some brain-teasers that will keep you busy for quite a long time. You will need a pencil and paper for a few of them and most of the puzzles have correct solutions on pages 28-35—but try not to look for them until you have worked the puzzles out for yourself.

JOINING THE RINGS

Here are nine rings all linked together by six

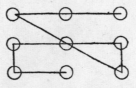

straight lines. Can you join them together, instead, by only *four* straight lines ?

HOW DID THE EGG GET INTO THE BOTTLE ?

You may have seen model ships in glass bottles and wondered how they got there. Well, here is a bottle mystery that you can prepare to puzzle your friends.

Soak an ordinary hen's egg in vinegar for several hours, until it is soft, then push it, whole, into a narrow-necked bottle. When it is safely inside pour in a solution of ammonium carbonate (you can buy this for about a penny at the chemist's) and wait until the egg slowly regains its shape and hardness.

STRANGE ARITHMETIC

Can you show that four added to six will make eleven ?

HIDDEN NUTS

During the autumn squirrels collect so many nuts that one larder is not big enough to hold them all, and so they each have several larders. Unfortunately

the squirrel hasn't a very good memory, and often forgets where some of his larders are ; then begins a great hunt to find the hidden nuts, and now you are going to have a hunt for some nuts too.

See if you can rearrange the jumbled letters below, so that each group spells the name of a nut.

EHZLA BOC
NALUTW LONDAM
ARBLIZ NUCCOOT
TOYKNUEMN RIBFELT
HUNTETCS TAPISOICH
CHEEB

CAGING THE LION

Draw a lion and a cage, as shown here. Now put a small card—a visiting card will do—upon the line

A–B, holding it upright. Put your face so close that the right eye looks upon the lion, whilst the left can see only the cage, and you will see the lion walk into the cage.

TASTING THE PLUM PUDDING

Sixty-four Christmas puddings are each offering you a bite, but the bite must be bitten in the correct way ! Starting at one of the two puddings with holly on top, you must go from pudding to pudding, never crossing a path you have taken before and never

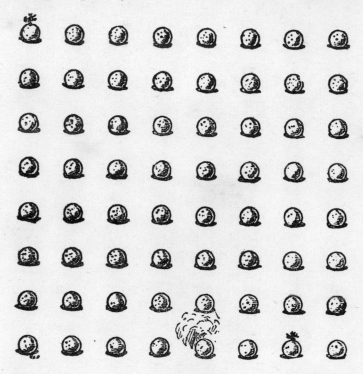

going over the same ground twice, finally reaching the other holly-bedecked pudding.

Take a pencil and see if you can find the right track.

THE PEARL-NECKLACE PUZZLE

On page 15 is a necklace of 33 pearls. The middle pearl is the largest and the best of all, and the others are so arranged that starting from one end each successive pearl is worth £100 more than the previous one, right up to the big pearl. From the other end the

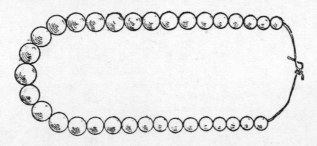

pearls increase in value by £150 up to the largest. The whole string is worth £65,000. What is the value of that large pearl?

SUGAR PROBLEM

This is a clever little problem which can be introduced at tea-time. Place three empty teacups on a table and put ten lumps of sugar in them so that there is an odd number of lumps in every cup. This sounds impossible, but it can be done. You'd better work it out with buttons or beads, as the sugar will probably be grubby by the time you've found the solution!

FIND THE WAY HOME

Have you ever tried to grope your way home in a dense fog when familiar roads seem as strange and misleading as Darkest Africa?

Try to find your way to the house in the puzzle on the following page. Imagine that the bus has

put you down at one of the side spaces, then set
out along the road towards the house. You must not
cheat by climbing any walls, and if you find yourself
in a blind alley you must go back and find another
way. A word of warning—it is quite a long walk!

16

OPTICAL ILLUSIONS

The "house" part of this Noah's Ark has been covered with invisible paint so that it cannot be seen, but study the roof and the hull closely. Would the fishes' journey from A to C be very much longer than the flies' walk from B to D?

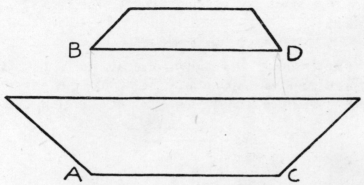

Let's pretend that these two diagrams are pictures of herrings' skeletons! One is swimming to the left and the other to the right. Would you say that their backbones are straight?

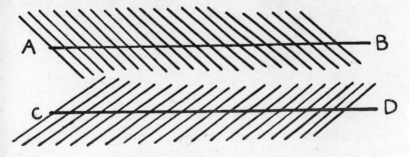

ELECTRIFIED BALLOONS

Ordinary toy balloons may be "electrified" by stroking them for a short time with a piece of fur.

After this treatment place one against the wall, or on the ceiling, and it will be found to stay there, as though stuck to it.

If you take two balloons which have been "electrified" and hang them up from the same point by means of silken threads you will be surprised to see that instead of sticking together they repel each other.

THE SEVEN PIGS

An Irishman was shown a square pen containing 7 pigs and was asked how he would intersect the pen with three straight fences so as to enclose every

pig in a separate sty. In other words, all you have to do is to take your pencil and with 3 straight strokes across the square, enclose each pig separately. Can you do it?

SIX NINES

Can you arrange six 9's in such a way that they add up to 100?

DRAUGHTSBOARD PUZZLE

Can you arrange eight men on a draughtsboard in such a way that no two are upon the same line in any direction?

CLOCK NUMBERS

Can you write down, in Roman figures, the numbers as they appear on a clock face? Be very stern with yourself over this! Do not look at the clock until you have finished—and then see how many of your figures are written the right way up.

MATCH PUZZLE

These sixteen squares are enclosed by sixteen matchsticks. The problem is to place an *odd* number

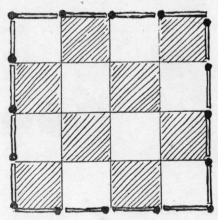

of matchsticks inside the square so as to enclose four groups of four squares each.

There are easy ways of doing this with 8, 10, or 12 matchsticks, but these are *even* numbers, and the problem is to use *odd* numbers of sticks.

You must not, of course, duplicate the matchsticks—that is, put one on top of another, or one alongside another.

A SUM FROM THE ZOO

An inquisitive boy who was on a visit to a small zoo asked the keeper how many animals and birds were to be seen there. He had asked so many questions already that the keeper decided to set him a poser.

"Well," he replied, "there are thirty-six heads and a hundred feet between the lot."

It took the inquisitive one quite a long time to work out the answer. Do you know what it was ?

MYSTERY OF THE EIGHT COUNTERS

Place eight counters or tiddlywinks of two different colours in a row, the colours alternating (as top line of the diagram). The puzzle is to arrange them as

shown in the second line, with all those of one colour together. Two neighbouring counters of the same or different colours must be moved at a time and placed in line with the others and touching them. You must make the change in four moves.

KNOTTY PROBLEM

Fold your handkerchief diagonally into a long strip and place it on the table in front of you.

Then, picking up one end in each hand, tie the handkerchief in a single knot—without releasing your hold of either end.

BOTTLING THE COIN

Bend an ordinary matchstick in two, partly breaking it, in such a way that the two parts hold together by a few fibres of the wood. Now place

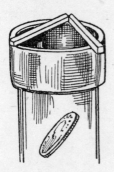

the match on the neck of a bottle, as shown here, and on the match place a sixpence or other small coin.

Now see if you can make the coin fall into the bottle without touching or blowing on the match, the bottle, or the coin, and without jerking the table.

PENNY POSER

Place three pennies in a row on the table so that they touch each other. Now try to move the left-hand penny away from the others without touching it in any way.

DIVIDE THE LAND

A farmer wished to sell some land which was laid out in nine plots in the shape of a cross, as shown here. He offered first choice of the plots to the first would-be purchaser who could so arrange the numbers

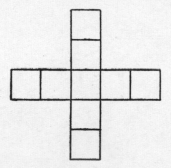

from 1 to 9 on the plots that they added up to 23 in all directions.

How would *you* have done it?

PAT'S PARTY

Our friend Pat gave a party
　　Upon St. Patrick's Day.
But who was there and what they did
　　I'll leave you now to say.
If you would solve the puzzle
　　And all words quickly see,
Remember that each answer
　　Begins with P—A—T.

1. What led to Pat's door.
2. The guard who stood outside.
3. What the guests had to have while they waited for the day of the party.
4. The oldest and most honoured guest.
5. What the poorest guest had on his shoe.

6. What leather Pat's shoes were made of.
7. The guest who was too ill to come.
8. What kind of stories they told about the ill man.
9. The guest who was most loyal to his country.
10. The favourite biscuits.

THE WIZARD'S CATS

A wizard placed ten cats inside a magic circle, as shown here, and hypnotised them so that they should remain stationary during his pleasure. He then drew three circles inside the large circle so that no cat could approach another cat without crossing a magic circle.

Try to draw the three circles so that every cat has its own enclosure and cannot reach another cat without crossing a line.

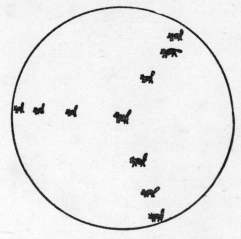

Solutions to puzzles are on pages 28–33.

WORD PUZZLES

HERE are a few " word " puzzles of various kinds.
They are fairly simple to work out and, what is
more, you can easily make up others on similar lines.

WORD SQUARES

These are made up of words each containing the
same number of letters. When the words are written
one below the other they spell the same words
horizontally and vertically, for example :

```
R E B E L
E V A D E
B A D G E
E D G E D
L E E D S
```

Clues are provided, from which the words have to
be guessed. The clues for the above are : 1, To
oppose the power of the Government. 2, To elude.
3, Mark or sign by which a person or object is dis-
tinguished. 4, Something having sharp, cutting parts.
5, A city in England.

See if you can solve this word square, and then
try to make some others.

1, A domain. 2, Nest of an eagle. 3, Part of an
amphitheatre. 4, A textile. 5, Signifies.

24

LADDER WORDS

In these teasers you are asked to change one word into another in so many moves, changing one letter at a time. For instance, to change DOG into RAT in three moves you can do this :

D O G
D O T
R O T
R A T

Now change MICE into CATS and BIRD into CAGE, each in four moves.

CROSSWORDS

Have you ever thought of compiling your own crossword puzzles? It is easy enough, when once you know how to set about it, and all you need is pencil, paper, a dictionary, and a reasonable amount of patience !

Start with a small puzzle measuring, say, nine squares wide and nine squares deep. Draw it on your paper, then fill in a design of blacks. These should be arranged so that no word, or group of words, is completely cut off from the rest of the puzzle. You should also be careful to see that there are not too many long words.

Decide first which long words you will use, as these form the framework of the puzzle. Then fit in the shorter words, making sure that their letters cross with words running the other way. When your puzzle is filled in with words, number them carefully. Then look in the dictionary for their definitions, on which you will base your clues.

When you have written out the clues and also the solution, rub out the words in the puzzle and put it

aside for a friend to solve—or you can paste it into a book to amuse yourself sometime when you have forgotten the solution !

And now for a ready-made crossword. Although there is only one diagram, there are three sets of clues. Solve clues " A " first, in light pencil, then erase your solution and go on to clues " B " and " C."

PUZZLE "A"

CLUES ACROSS	CLUES DOWN
1. Small quadruped.	1. Indian coin.
7. A sailor.	2. Fairy queen.
8. Point of the compass.	3. With ability.
9. Dignity.	4. Hotels.
13. Period after Christ.	5. Sheltered side.
14. Affirmative.	6. To eject with force.
15. That thing.	10. Poem.
16. Prefix meaning "in."	11. A fish.
18. Great (ab.).	12. Rest.
20. Exclamation.	17. At no time.
22. Bachelor of laws.	18. Dazzling light.
24. Talk wildly.	19. Native of Arabia.
25. Organs of hearing.	21. Warmth.
26. One who eats.	22. Beverage.
28. Those who traffic by exchange.	23. The Thames at Oxford.
	27. Number curtailed.

PUZZLE "B"

CLUES ACROSS	CLUES DOWN
1. Enchanted place.	1. To drop down.
7. First class.	2. Boy's name.
8. Account.	3. Pile or heap.
9. English town.	4. To endure.
13. Lid curtailed.	5. A deed.
14. Outfit.	6. Defence of Realm Act (ab.).
15. Note in the sol-fa scale.	10. Atmosphere.
16. Resident magistrate (ab.).	11. To be unwell.
18. French measurement.	12. A tree.
20. Exclamation.	17. Kind of tooth.
22. To perform.	18. Reptile.
24. Girl's name.	19. Girl's name.
25. Kind of goat.	21. Circle of light.
26. Found in a church.	22. Part of a clock.
28. Method of travelling.	23. Part of a car.
	27. With nothing makes the top.

PUZZLE "C"

CLUES ACROSS

1. French national heroine.
7. That is.
8. Two-thirds of a donkey.
9. Symbol of good luck.
13. North America (ab.).
14. Dangerous explosive.
15. Pronoun.
16. Britain's sure shield (ab.).
18. Verb.
20. Before noon.
22. Point of the compass.
24. Gown.
25. Saint said to be connected with fishermen.
26. Kind of window.
28. Pass in the Alps.

CLUES DOWN

1. A king of England.
2. Essential to life.
3. Bird's home.
4. Secure.
5. Hard wood tree.
6. Indian tribe.
10. Used in boating.
11. Farthest from the beginning.
12. To be in debt.
17. Native Indian ruler.
18. Girl's name.
19. Greek god.
21. Lake.
22. Observed.
23. A dye.
27. Decapitated knight.

PUZZLE SOLUTIONS

JOINING THE RINGS

The rings can be joined by four straight lines as shown in this diagram :

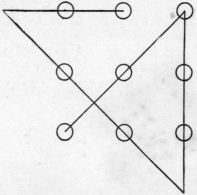

STRANGE ARITHMETIC

Write IV turned upside down below VI and the answer is XI.

HIDDEN NUTS

Hazel, walnut, brazil, monkeynut, chestnut, beech, cob, almond, coconut, filbert, pistachio.

TASTING THE PLUM PUDDING

If you taste the puddings in the order shown here you will not visit any pudding twice, or cross any line.

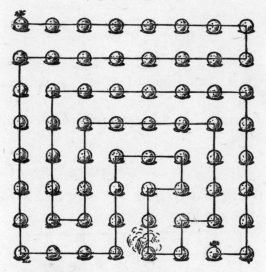

THE PEARL NECKLACE

The value of the large centre pearl is £3,000. The pearl at one end (from which they increase in value by £100) is worth £1,400 ; the pearl at the other end is worth £600.

SUGAR PROBLEM

Place one lump of sugar in the first cup, two lumps in the second, and seven in the third. Then place

the first cup in the second cup, as shown in the diagram, and the second cup will then be holding three lumps of sugar—an odd number.

OPTICAL ILLUSIONS

The fishes and the flies would have the same distance to travel, for lines BD and AC are exactly the same length.

The herrings' backbones are parallel and quite straight.

THE SEVEN PIGS

The sketch shows how the pigs can be separated by three straight lines.

SIX NINES

$$99\frac{99}{99} = 100.$$

DRAUGHTSBOARD PUZZLE

Here is one solution. Place a man on the first square of the fifth line ; the second square of the second line ; third of the fourth line ; fourth of the sixth line ; fifth of the eighth line ; sixth of the third line ; seventh of the first line, and eighth of the seventh line.

MATCH PUZZLE

The illustration shows one of the four different ways of solving the puzzle, with eleven, an *odd* number

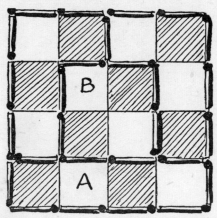

of match sticks. If you first enclose an outside row, as A, then you can enclose the square, B, in any position, and complete the solution with eleven matches in all.

A SUM FROM THE ZOO

Thirty-six birds would have 72 feet, which were too few ; thirty-six beasts would total 144 feet—44 too many. Eighteen of each would give 108 feet—8 too many. Subtract four beasts and add four birds : Fourteen beasts would have 56 feet ; twenty-two birds would have 44 feet ; 56 + 44 = 100.

KNOTTY PROBLEM

Fold your arms, stoop over the table, and pick up each end of the handkerchief. Unfold your arms slowly, retaining your hold on the hanky, and a knot will be tied.

BOTTLING THE COIN

Dip your finger in a glass of water, and placing it above the angle formed by the match, allow one or

two drops of water to fall on it. Immediately the fibres of the wood will try to straighten themselves, and the angle will increase little by little until the match no longer supports the coin, which then drops into the bottle.

PENNY POSER

Place your left forefinger firmly on the centre penny. Then, with your right forefinger, knock the right-hand penny sharply against the centre coin. The left-hand penny will move away with the force of the impact.

DIVIDE THE LAND

Here is one solution :

$$8$$
$$3$$
$$9\ 2\ 1\ 4\ 7$$
$$5$$
$$6$$

PAT'S PARTY

These words, all beginning with " P A T " help to tell you what happened at the party :

Path, patrol, patience, patriarch, patch, patent, patient, pathetic, patriot, pat-a-cake.

THE WIZARD'S CATS

The illustration on page 34 shows clearly how the three circles may be drawn so that every cat has a separate enclosure, and cannot approach another cat without crossing a magic line.

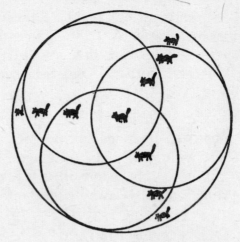

WORD SQUARE

R E A L M
E Y R I E
A R E N A
L I N E N
M E A N S

LADDER WORDS

M I C E   B I R D
M A C E   B A R D
M A T E   B A R E
M A T S   C A R E
C A T S   C A G E

CROSSWORDS

A

Across.—1, Armadillo. 7, A.B. 8, N.E. 9, Nobleness. 13, A.D. 14, Yes. 15, It. 16, En.

18, Gt. 20, Eh. 22, B.L. 24, Rave. 25, Ears. 26, Eater. 28, Barterers.

Down.—1, Anna. 2, Mab. 3, Ably. 4, Inns. 5, Lee. 6, Oust. 10, Ode. 11, Eel. 12, Sit. 17, Never. 18, Glare. 19, Arab. 21, Heat. 22, Beer. 23, Isis. 27, Te.

B

Across.—1, Fairyland. 7, A.I. 8, A.C. 9, Lancaster. 13, Li. 14, Kit. 15, La. 16, R.M. 18, Cm. (cetnimetre). 20, Oh. 22, Do. 24, Ella. 25, Ibex. 26, Altar. 28, Aeroplane.

Down.—1, Fall. 2, Ian. 3, Rick. 4, Last. 5, Act. 6, D.O.R.A. 10, Air. 11, Ail. 12, Elm. 17, Molar. 18, Cobra. 19, Lena. 21, Halo. 22, Dial. 23, Axle. 27, Tp.

C

Across.—1, Joan of Arc. 7, I.e. 8, As. 9, Horseshoe. 13, N.A. 14, T.N.T. 15, We. 16, R.N. (Royal Navy). 18, Be. 20, A.m. 22, S.E. 24, Robe. 25, Elmo. 26, Oriel. 28, St. Bernard.

Down.—1, John. 2, Air. 3, Nest. 4, Fast. 5, Ash. 6, Cree. 10, Oar. 11, End. 12, Owe. 17, Nabob. 18, Bella. 19, Eros. 21, Mere. 22, Seen. 23, Woad. 27, Ir.

FUN WITH THE GRAMOPHONE

HAVE you ever thought of the interesting things you can do with a gramophone besides playing records on it ? With the parental permission, of course !

Here are some experiments that you might like

FIG. I.

to try, and all you need for them is a supply of drawing-paper or thin card, a pair of compasses, a pencil, and a fair amount of patience.

First of all cut out five circles of card, each six inches in diameter. If you have no gramophone and wish to try out the experiments with a spinning-pencil, the circle should be smaller. In each case make a hole in the centre after you have drawn the designs.

36

Start with the "Vanishing Spirals." Draw three curved lines on one disc as shown in Fig. 1. One line must be black, another blue, and the third red. Having pierced a hole in the centre, spin the disc on the gramophone turntable and the lines will seem to move towards the centre of the circle and disappear.

Now for the "Rolling Circles." There are two designs for this experiment and they are shown in

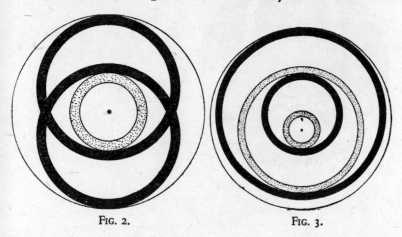

FIG. 2.   FIG. 3.

Figs. 2 and 3. For Fig. 2 describe two large circles which cut one another and enclose a small circle concentric with the disc. Use different colours for each circle to get the best effect, and you will see the larger circles moving round the small one.

In Fig. 3 describe two pairs of circles about two centres, neither of which is the centre of the disc. Study the illustration and this will be clear to you. Then watch the effect when it is spun.

When you have amused yourself for a while with

these you may like to try another. The "Wriggling Line" is fascinating to watch. The disc you will use for this is shown in Fig. 4. If you fix your eyes on a point of this as it revolves, the white line will seem to wriggle in a strange way.

To enable you to draw this design accurately a diagram (Fig. 5) is given. The dotted curves are

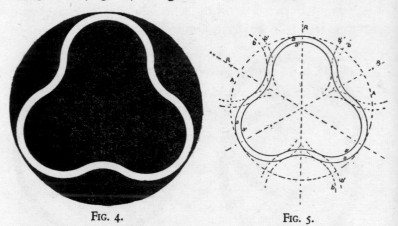

FIG. 4.   FIG. 5.

Geometrically-minded readers may prefer to use the right-hand diagram as a guide to the "wriggling-line" shown above. Or it can be traced on to your disc from this illustration.

those parts of the circles which do not enter into the design. The big circle A is the disc which you may have already cut out (in this case pin it to a sheet of paper for steadiness). The circumference of this is divided into six equal parts (chord equal to radius), and through the points of division are drawn the six lines from the centre. Describe circles *a a a*, each half the diameter of A. The circles *b b b* are then drawn from centres on the lines R R R, and with the same radius as *a a a*. The same centres are used for describing the circles a' a' a' and b' b' b', parts of which form the inner boundary of the line. The background should be blackened and the belt be left white.

After this try the "Disappearing Circles," the design for which is shown in Fig. 6. Two sets of circles are described about different centres, and the crescent-shaped areas between them are coloured, the remainder of the disc being left white. When you spin this by its true centre on the gramophone you

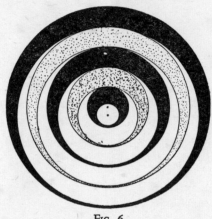

FIG. 6.

will get the impression that the coloured parts are portions of different discs separated by white discs.

Now for the sixth experiment, "Rainbow," for which you will need a disc only four inches across. This one is very suitable for spinning on a pencil.

Blacken one half of the disc, as shown in Fig. 7. On the other half draw four series of concentric black lines. When this is spun with a clockwise rotation (as on a gramophone turntable) the outermost lines seem to be greenish blue, those nearest the centre

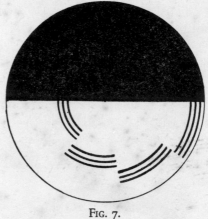

FIG. 7.

dark red, and the intermediate groups yellow and green.

When the disc is spun in an anti-clockwise direction (this time on a pencil), the order of the colours is reversed. You will have the best results from this experiment if you try it by artificial light.

COOKING

A chapter to remember when rationing is forgotten

OF all the things you can do when you have to stay indoors by yourself, one of the most interesting is cooking.

Now, cooking is not something that only girls can do—or *want* to do ! Boys, too, will find it amusing to make sweets and try to cook simple dishes for themselves—a most useful accomplishment when you go camping in the summer !

Mothers, and grown-ups in general, are apt to frown upon juvenile cooking experiments, regarding them as unnecessary evils that always entail saucepan marks on the table and all kinds of indescribable stickinesses on the stove. But not so. If you are careful to see that nothing boils over and no fat splashes from the frying pan and, what is more, clear everything up when you have finished, your culinary enterprises will be regarded with a more favourable eye, and someone might even be persuaded to eat something you have cooked. That is the supreme reward.

For your first effort at making sweets you may like to try these old favourites :

TOFFEE APPLES

Ingredients : 4 oz. butter, 1 lb. Demerara sugar, ½ tablespoonful vinegar. Some medium-sized apples.

Boil the butter, sugar, and vinegar together without stirring until, when you drop a little into a saucer of cold water, it becomes crisp at once. Remove the saucepan from the heat. Push a wooden skewer, or other smooth stick, through each apple, dip the apples in the toffee so that they are well coated, and stand them by the sticks in jam jars to harden.

COCONUT CANDY

Ingredients : 1 lb. desiccated coconut, 1 pint milk, 4 tablespoonfuls black treacle (or golden syrup), 1 tablespoonful butter.

Boil the milk, treacle, and butter together for ten minutes, stirring carefully. Then add the coconut. Try a piece of the mixture in a saucer of cold water. If it sets, tip the contents of the saucepan into a buttered tin. If not, cook a little longer until it *does* set. When the candy becomes cold cut it into bars.

PEPPERMINT DROPS

Ingredients : ¾ lb. granulated sugar, 8 drops oil of peppermint, 4 tablespoonfuls boiling water.

Put the sugar and water into a strong saucepan and stir until the sugar is dissolved and boiling. Now stop stirring and boil the mixture until a small sample can be moulded to a soft ball when you drop it into a saucer of cold water. Then remove the saucepan from the heat, stir in the peppermint and beat until it is white and creamy. Then spread out some grease-proof or wax paper, drop small blobs of the mixture on to it from a teaspoon and leave them to set.

BLACKCURRANT BRITTLE

Ingredients : 3 tablespoonfuls blackcurrant jam, 1 pint water, some brown sugar.

Dissolve the jam in the water and boil together for three minutes. Place a sieve over a basin and pass the mixture through. Measure the liquid in the basin and place it, with twice its bulk of brown sugar in a well-greased saucepan. Boil, stirring occasionally, until a small drop sets quite hard in a saucer of cold water. Then turn the contents of the saucepan into a greased tin and leave it to harden. Mark it into bars or squares with a knife when it is nearly set.

NOTE.—To clean saucepans that have been used for sweet-making, use very hot water. If necessary, soak the saucepan for half an hour or so.

Now for a few simple dishes

When you think of something that is easy to cook, your mind immediately turns towards eggs, so here are a few ways of cooking them.

BOILED EGGS

This is the very easiest way. If you have never boiled an egg before you should know that three and a half minutes is the time it takes to cook it to suit the average taste. That is, if you place the egg in boiling water. If you put the egg in a saucepan of cold water, allow it one and a half minute's cooking after the water has come to the boil. It is wise to use an enamelled saucepan, as egg-boiling often stains aluminium.

(240)

43

4

FRIED EGGS

Melt some lard or dripping in a frying pan, break the egg and drop it in. As the white begins to set slip the blade of a knife under the edges to prevent it sticking to the pan. When the yolk starts setting pour a little of the hot fat over it, using a spoon. Take the egg from the pan very carefully with a broad knife or an egg-slice.

SCRAMBLED EGGS

Melt a little margarine in a small saucepan. When it starts bubbling add a good tablespoonful of milk and into this stir a well-beaten egg with a little salt and pepper. Keep stirring until the mixture begins to get solid, then turn it out and eat at once, preferably on toast.

POACHED EGGS

This is a very easy way if you have a proper poaching pan, with little cups for the eggs. If not, you can use a fairly deep patty pan (placed in a frying pan), or a cup in a saucepan. In any case, fill your poacher or saucepan with water, or half-fill the frying pan. Bring to the boil. Grease whatever receptacle you are using for the egg, drop the egg in it, place it in the pan and cook until it is set. A poached egg, too, is nicest eaten on toast.

PANCAKES

Quite a lot of people seem to think that Shrove Tuesday is the only day in all the year when pancakes should be eaten, but they are so delicious that if you had one every day it would not be too often ! You can make several pancakes quite easily from this recipe.

Ingredients : 4 oz. self-raising flour, $\frac{1}{4}$ pint milk, $\frac{1}{4}$ pint water, 1 egg, pinch of salt, some lard for frying and also a little lemon juice.

Mix the flour and salt together in a basin, make a little well in the middle and break the egg into it. Start to mix the flour lightly into the egg, starting at the centre and gradually working through. Then mix the milk and water together and add slowly, beating the mixture well as you do so. Continue to beat until the batter becomes smooth and lots of little air bubbles rise in it. Stand the basin aside for at least an hour.

Melt a little lard in a frying pan and pour some of the batter into it so that the bottom of the pan is thinly coated. As it begins to set and cook lift the edges with an egg-slice or broad knife so that the pancake does not stick. It will soon cook on one side and then you must turn it. Really experienced cooks simply toss their pancakes by taking the pan from the fire, giving it a flip and—hey presto ! the pancake comes down the other way up. But this takes practice and your pancake may stick to the ceiling, so turn it instead very carefully with the egg-slice by folding it over gradually.

When the pancake is a nice golden brown on both sides, turn it out on to sugared paper, sprinkle lemon juice and more sugar on it, fold it sides to middle and eat at once.

WELSH RAREBIT

Ingredients : 1 oz. margarine, 2 oz. grated cheese, half cup milk, 1 egg, pepper and salt to taste, $\frac{1}{2}$ teaspoonful made mustard.

First make some toast, butter it and set aside to keep hot. Then melt the margarine in a small saucepan. When bubbling add the milk and cheese and stir until the cheese is dissolved. Add the seasoning and mustard and then the well-beaten egg. Stir it all together until the mixture starts to set. Now spread it on the toast and place it under the grill for a few minutes until it browns nicely on top.

Now for some cakes

By the time you have tried these recipes you will begin to feel your feet in the kitchen, so you may like to make some cakes. Here are some that are fairly easy. No oven is required for the Crunchies, but for the others you must arrange matters so that the oven will be at the right temperature by the time the cakes are ready to be put in. As there are many types of ovens it is not possible to tell you how to adjust the heat, but a popular test of the heat is to put a sheet of white paper into the oven, and if it has turned a good yellow colour by the end of five minutes there is sufficient heat to bake a cake.

Once the moisture has been added to the flour the sooner the cake is in the oven the better, so have your oven ready and your tins greased before you begin mixing.

CHOCOLATE CRUNCHIES

Ingredients : A bar of milk chocolate and some corn flakes.

Melt the chocolate by putting it in a small basin and placing this in a saucepan of water over the gas. When it has melted, remove from the heat and drop two or three tablespoonfuls of corn flakes into the basin. See that the flakes are well coated with chocolate, then lift out in teaspoonfuls and set in a safe place to dry. They look very appetising when they are put into small paper cake cases.

FAIRYCAKES

Ingredients (for about ten cakes) : 3 oz. self-raising flour, 2 oz. margarine, 2 oz. caster sugar, 1 egg, a little milk ; 1 oz. currants, if liked.

Warm the margarine slightly in the mixing bowl, add the sugar, and beat them both together until the mixture becomes really soft and creamy. Then add the beaten egg and stir well. Next add the flour (sifted, if possible) and, before mixing it in, the currants. Now mix all together very lightly, add a very little milk if the mixture is stiff. It should be moist enough to drop fairly easily from the spoon.

Half fill some small cake tins, or paper cases—which do not require greasing—with the cake mixture. Bake in a moderately hot oven for 15 to 20 minutes. Resist the temptation to look at your cakes before ten minutes are up or they will be spoilt.

LITTLE CHOCOLATE CAKES

Ingredients : 1 egg and its weight in margarine, caster sugar, and self-raising flour, 1 tablespoonful of cocoa powder.

Mix your ingredients together in the same way as for Fairy Cakes, adding the cocoa with the flour. Cook these cakes also in a moderate oven for 15 to 20 minutes.

JAM TARTS

Ingredients : 4 oz. self-raising flour, 2 oz. margarine, a pinch of salt, and a little water. Jam, marmalade, or lemon-curd.

First make the pastry by mixing together the flour and salt. Then cut the margarine into small pieces and rub it into the flour with the tips of your fingers until it is as fine as breadcrumbs. Add small quantities of water until you have a fairly soft dough, but be careful not to make it too moist.

Sprinkle some flour on the pastry board and also the rolling-pin. Turn the dough on to the board and roll it out lightly until it is a little less than a quarter of an inch thick. Cut it into rounds to fit your tart tins with the aid of a pastry cutter or the top of a tumbler. Place in the greased tins.

Into each tart drop a teaspoonful of jam, marmalade, or lemon-curd. Bake in a moderately hot oven until the pastry begins to turn golden brown. This should take about 10 to 15 minutes.

A word of warning : be sparing with the jam, or as it cooks, it will bubble up all over the pastry and turn into " toffee " on the tins. You can always add more jam when the tarts are finished. Another way is to put a little rice into the pastry cases instead (to keep them flat at the bottom) ; then, when they are cooked, you simply tip out the rice and put in the jam.

BACHELOR'S BUTTONS

Ingredients: 5 oz. self-raising flour, 3 oz. caster sugar, 2 oz. butter or margarine, 1 egg, a little flavouring.

Mix the butter and sugar as for fairycakes, then beat the egg and flavouring and add it gradually with the flour until a stiffish paste is formed. Do not add all the egg unless it is necessary. Take small pieces of the mixture, and roll them into balls the size of a hazel nut, using a little flour on the hands to prevent them sticking. Place the biscuits on a greased tin, and when all are ready sprinkle with a little sugar. (To prepare the tin, first grease it and then sprinkle on a little flour, knock the edges of the tin on the table, so that the flour covers the whole surface of the tin, then shake off any surplus flour.)

Bake in a good oven until the biscuits are lightly browned ; this will take about 12 minutes. Then lift them off the tin on to a sieve or wire tray to cool.

MAKING MODELS AND TOYS

THIS is a pastime that will keep you busy for hours—and the result will be a fine collection of playthings.

A MERRY-GO-ROUND

Take a piece of stiff paper about two feet square and fold it three times, first in halves, as in Fig. 1 ; then, with the folded edge towards you, in three parts, by laying the left half of the edge on the right

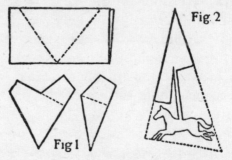

Fig. 2

Fig 1

dotted line and by laying the right half of the folded edge on the left dotted line, now covered ; then in halves again. Cut off the top part along the dotted line.

Draw the lines and the horse indicated in Fig. 2, then cut carefully along the lines, open the paper and press it flat, as in Fig. 3. Cut off the horses that are facing the wrong way and the pieces marked X ; cut

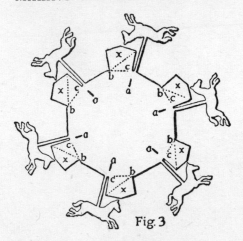

Fig. 3

along the lines *b–c* and cut the slits *a*. That makes the wings.

Cut a round of cardboard the size of the large circle, paste it on the under side of the paper and

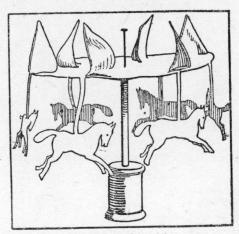

The finished model.

stick a pin through the centre and into a pencil. Push the other end of the pencil into an empty reel, as large

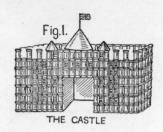

Fig.1.

THE CASTLE

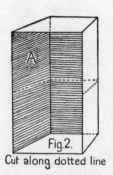

A

Fig.2.

Cut along dotted line

Fig.3.

WINDOWS

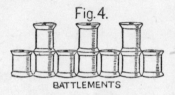

Fig.4.

BATTLEMENTS

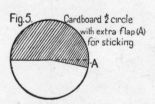

Fig.5. Cardboard ½ circle
with extra flap (A)
for sticking.

A

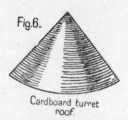

Fig.6.

Cardboard turret
roof.

Fig.7.

GATEWAY

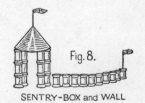

Fig. 8.

SENTRY-BOX and WALL

as possible, bend down the horses and blow gently into the " wings," and the merry-go-round will spin.

A COTTON-REEL CASTLE

A splendid castle can be made from empty cotton-reels, an ordinary boot-box, and some cardboard. Your finished castle will appear as in Fig. 1.

First take the boot-box and cut it in half (Fig. 2). The part marked A will form the outline of the courtyard. Having marked some of the reels for windows (Fig. 3), proceed to build the castle, adapting it according to the number of reels you have been able to collect, remembering that the top row must have gaps so as to appear " battlemented " (Fig. 4).

Build up a central tower and side turrets of reels, cap them with roofs made of cardboard half-circles (Figs. 5 and 6). For the top of the large central tower a paper flag, on which you have painted the Union Jack, can float from a long pin. Place ordinary tin soldiers on guard.

If you have not enough reels for such a large model as the castle, thirty-three will make a castle gateway, with the help of a piece of cardboard (Fig. 7). Or twenty-two will make a sentry-box and wall, if a cardboard turret made as in Figs. 5 and 6 be glued to the top (Fig. 8). The models can be stuck together with tube-glue, or if you only want the reels built up temporarily they can be held together with little dabs of modelling clay, or play-wax.

BALANCING TOYS

All sorts of birds and animals that will sit on a piece of taut string or the edge of a bowl or even on your finger, can be made from post cards.

Trace the outlines, shown here and transfer them on to the card, either with carbon paper, or else by putting the pencilled side of the tracing downwards

and rubbing the back all over with a soft pencil. Colour the figures on both sides, and when quite dry carefully cut out. Then put a paper-clip as a weight on the tail at the point marked A, and the figure will sit up if gently placed in position, point B being the resting point.

If you like to make more permanent ornaments you can do so by mounting the tracings on to ply-wood and cutting them out with a fret-saw. If you decided to do this you will be able to paint them with Japanese lacquer, cellulose, or other quick-drying paints, and get splendid results. The figures can easily be enlarged, as long as care is taken to get the points A and B in a straight line, which is the secret of the balancing.

A FLUTTER RING

A flutter ring that you can put in an envelope as a surprise for one of your friends is a very amusing thing to make. By looking at the picture you can see how easy it is. The frame is made from a piece of wire eight inches long, two inches of which at each end are bent at right angles. Bend over the wire at its extreme ends in the form of little hooks. The ring

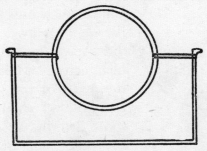

may be about two inches across, and should be of stout wire, or, if it can be obtained, a key-ring would do very well. The ring must have an opening somewhere, as two short rubber bands have to be attached to it without cutting.

Slip the rubber bands over the ring, and attach one to each hook. Now twist the ring round and round on the rubber bands as an axis until they are very tight. Fold the whole thing in a piece of paper, and then enclose in an envelope. You must keep a good hold of the ring all the time to prevent it untwisting whilst you are wrapping it up.

Give the envelope to someone, and say that it contains a surprise. When the flutter ring is revealed it causes much surprise by starting to revolve rapidly. Quite likely your friend will drop the thing in his astonishment, and then it jumps about all over the floor just as if it were alive.

DARING YOUNG MAN ON A BUBBLE BALLOON

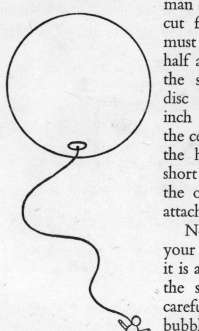

Did you know that a bubble will carry a little man ? The figure should be cut from tissue paper, and it must not be more than about half an inch high. Now from the same paper cut a small disc about an eighth of an inch across. Make a hole in the centre of this, and through the hole knot one end of a short length of cotton. To the other end of the cotton attach the man.

Now you must blow up your soap bubble and, when it is a fair size, soak the disc in the soap solution. Put this carefully on to one side of the bubble and it will slide round to the lowest part.

Of course you must not touch the bubble with your fingers, or it would certainly burst. The disc, being wet with the soap solution, does not harm the bubble in any way. Jerk the bubble free from the pipe, and away it sails with the little figure attached.

Instead of a figure you might cut out a shape like a balloon car, and so make the bubble more than ever like a real balloon.

THE DYING FISH

You may have noticed that a dead fish floats on its back ? Well, a wooden fish can have the same peculiarity, as you will see if you make this toy.

Cut a piece of deal into a prism about four inches long, and colour two of the sides black or dark blue, painting the remaining side white.

Sharpen one end into a small triangular point, and paint two eyes and a mouth thereon, so that the completed fish appears as shown here.

Now, if you put this fish in a basin of water very heavily salted, you will find that the fish floats quite naturally. But if you place it in a basin of plain fresh water, he will immediately turn on his back and float " dead " with the white side uppermost.

A PAPER FISH THAT SWIMS

From a piece of ordinary notepaper cut out a fish like the one shown here, about seven or eight inches long. In the centre make a circular hole (A), and from it cut a narrow strip straight along to the tail (AB). Having done this, fill a long dish or bath with water, and place the fish on the surface in such

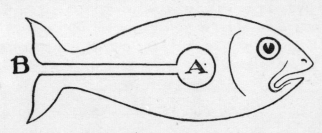

a way that the underneath surface is completely moistened, while the upper remains quite dry.

Now drop one large drop of oil into the opening A. The oil will immediately try to spread over the surface

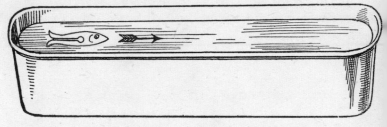

of the liquid, but that it can only do by escaping down the narrow passage to the tail.

This it does, and the fish swims forward.

A LOOSE-LEAF PICTURE BOOK

In magazines and newspapers there are often lots of interesting pictures which you would like to keep : if you just cut them out they are apt to get torn and lost, so the best thing to do is to paste them into a scrap-book.

Scrap-books with paper covers very soon come to pieces and good strong books are expensive to buy, so make a book for yourself ; it is quite simple. All that you need will be several sheets of strong brown paper, a thick cardboard box such as drapers use, a couple of yards of ribbon, not more than an inch wide, and some paste. (Paste can be made by putting a

dessertspoonful of plain flour into a breakfast cup, mixing it to a smooth cream with a little cold water, then adding boiling water and stirring until the mixture becomes half transparent. When cold it is ready for use.) A penny paste brush is also necessary.

The picture book shown here measures fifteen inches by twelve inches, and this is a very useful size, as the sheets of brown paper from which the pages are to be made will probably measure about forty-five inches by twenty-nine inches, which means you will get eight pages from one sheet. The lid of the draper's box will provide a sheet of cardboard for one cover, and the bottom of the box will provide the other. To cut them to the exact measurements, place the cardboard on the floor, or on an old deal-topped table, and having marked out the exact size with the help of a rule and a pencil, cut the cardboard along the lines with a sharply pointed penknife. Cover each piece of cardboard with a sheet of smooth thick brown paper, cut a couple of inches larger than the cardboard, folding it over neatly and mitreing the corners before pasting down all round the edges on the inside of the cover.

A second sheet of paper, cut an inch smaller than the cardboard, must be brushed over with paste for an inch all round the edge, and placed inside the cover to hide all the rough edges of paper and make the book look neat.

When the two covers have been finished, they should be put under a pile of books until the paste has had time to dry, and then slits wide enough to take the ribbon must be carefully cut in both covers. First of all measure and mark on each cover the exact spot where the slits are to come—an inch and a quarter from the left-hand edge and an inch and a half from the top and bottom edges are good positions. The slits must be cut very carefully or the cover will look untidy. It is a great improvement to place ties at the opposite ends of the covers also. For these a set of slits similar to the " hinge " slits must be cut in both the top and bottom covers.

The covers of the loose-leaf book are now ready,

and all that remains to do is to cut sheets of brown paper to the same size as the covers. Some people prefer the covers to be slightly larger than the pages, as a protection for the edges, but whatever size you decide to have the pages, the slits on the left-hand side must be in exactly the same position as they are in the cover, so that they may be tied into the book when the pictures have been pasted on to them. If the slits are cut in the pages *before* the pictures are pasted in, there is no fear of finding that a slit must be cut in one of the pictures.

When the pages are ready to be tied into the book, the top and bottom covers should be placed in position, with the pages arranged in their proper order in between, and a piece of ribbon about a yard and a quarter long must be passed through them, starting from the left-hand top corner slit in the front cover, through the pages and the back cover along the back, up through the pages to the front cover, where it comes through the left-hand lower corner slit. The two ends are then drawn together and tied in a bow.

The four short ties for the outer edges of the book consist of nine-inch lengths of ribbon, passed through each of the remaining four slits in the covers, from the inside to the outside. The ends inside the covers are rolled tightly once or twice to neaten them, thus making little flat rolls to prevent them from being pulled through when the book is tied up. These little rolls can have a stitch or two put in them if they show any signs of coming unrolled.

The decoration of the outside of the cover is a matter of choice. If you are collecting aeroplane pictures, probably you will want to have a colour picture of the most up-to-date 'plane you can find ; if you are specializing in animals you may like a good study of your favourite animal. The brown-paper background shows up any coloured decorations splendidly. If you are good at lettering, the words " Scrap Book " or " Picture Book " might be illuminated on the cover, using gold or silver paint, and introducing whatever colour you have chosen for the ribbon.

These picture books are very useful, and if you have any spare time and pictures to make extra books, you can be certain that any children's hospital will welcome them for the patients.

MAKE THE " FLYING MATCHBOX "

Materials needed : A few matchboxes, a number of pins, a sheet of thick notepaper, and some stout cardboard. A tube of adhesive and a few water-colour paints should also be obtained ; the glue for fastening the matchboxes together and the paints for colouring your model, and also for painting the carriage windows.

First of all get the matchboxes together ; then study Figs. 1, 2, 4, and 5. Each box has a cover (C) and a little drawer (D), which can be arranged as in Fig. 1 to form the upper and lower parts of a carriage—stick them together. The body of the tender (Fig. 4) is made by sticking two little drawers back to back, but one end of the upper box must be taken off. The " boiler " of the engine is made by gluing a piece of stout notepaper to a drawer turned upside down. In Fig. 5 you will see how the paper is to be bent round. In the same sketch the method of making the paper funnel and "windguard" is also shown.

The best way to make wheels is to place a farthing on a piece of stout cardboard, and then mark round

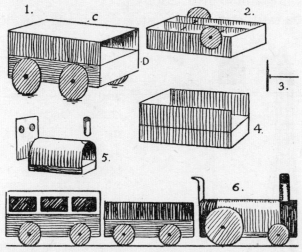

The "Flying Matchbox" ready for the iron road.

it with pencil. Cut out these wheels with a pair of sharp scissors.

Now look at Fig. 2 and you will see how you are to glue a little strip of cardboard under the drawer (right down the middle, as shown). The pins, which will be fixed through the exact middle of each wheel, must then be pushed through the sides of the drawer and into the middle piece of cardboard (clearly shown in Fig. 2). A tiny scrap of cardboard must be placed on each pin (as shown in Fig. 3) to keep the wheels from touching the wooden boxes. The driving wheels of the engine should be the size of a halfpenny.

MODEL OF THE EIFFEL TOWER

You have heard of the huge Eiffel Tower in Paris, and you can easily make a simplified model of it if you follow these instructions.

You will need a thick square of wood for the base

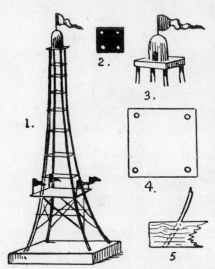

and four long thin strips about two or even three feet long and one-eighth inch thick. Bore four holes in the base block, one at each corner, to receive the ends of the four uprights. Cut the top platform out of cardboard, as shown in Fig. 2, whittle out the little house that stands on it and glue it in position (Fig. 3). The upper ends of the uprights fit into holes bored in this platform.

Then cut out, from thick cardboard, the middle platform. All four uprights pass through this by means of holes bored in its corners (Fig. 4). Now put a little glue in each of the holes in the base and push the bottom ends of the uprights into them (Fig. 5).

The cross-pieces and bracings are only flower-wire

(you can buy a reel of it for about twopence). The flags on the middle platform can be fixed to four long pins ; a match would make the top flagstaff. And, of course, the Tricolour must fly bravely from the top !

A WIRE SWITCHBACK

To make this amusing little toy you will need two strips of wood, a tiny block of wood, a matchbox, two matchsticks, some panel pins and a length of fairly thick wire.

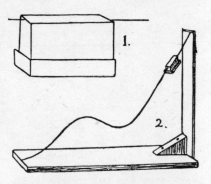

First of all make the tiny carriage for the switchback. Take the tray out of the match-box and into the case that is left glue two matchsticks. They should be spaced quarter of an inch apart along one of the narrow sides. Then glue the case, by the opposite narrow side, into the tray of the matchbox, as shown in Fig. 1.

Now fix your two strips of wood together at right angles, as shown in Fig. 2, with the tiny triangular block between them to hold them rigid. This fixing should be done with the panel pins, which can be obtained at any ironmonger's.

Next, push the wire through the carriage you have made so that it runs between the two matchsticks. Bend it realistically, then fix to the wooden frame at the bottom by means of bent pins. It should be just hooked over the upright one. Give the carriage a push and it will whizz merrily down the wire.

TOBOGGANNING IS GOOD SPORT !

A toboggan is a very useful thing to have. You can have endless fun on it, whizzing down snow-covered slopes, and quite a large amount of shopping,

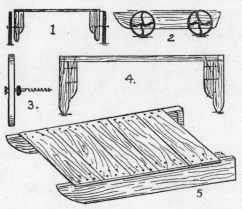

etc., can be piled on it and dragged easily along the road instead of being stowed heavily into a basket.

Get from a builder two pieces of wood, about four feet long and one inch thick. You will also want two other pieces a little shorter but of the same thickness. Also from the builder (or your grocer may have some boxes) get some smooth pieces of board, nearly half an inch thick.

Take two of the inch-thick boards for the runners and shape them as shown in Figs. 4 and 5. Fig. 4 shows how the strengthening pieces (one inch thick) are to be nailed or screwed inside the runners. Screwing is stronger.

Having made the runners, see that your smooth pieces of board are all exactly the same width. Cut them up into equal lengths, the width you want your toboggan to be, and nail or screw them to the runners. In Figs. 4 and 5 you will see just how the nails should be fixed. A double line of nails runs, you will notice, down each side of the top of the toboggan, so as to hold the boards very firmly to the runners and strengthening pieces.

Figs. 1, 2, and 3 show how little iron wheels can be screwed to the runners and strengthening pieces to make the toboggan into a go-cart, but you may prefer to leave these off. If you decide to have them, a long thin screw—two inches long at least—with a nut or washer threaded on to it to keep the wheel away from the runner, will be required for each wheel. You have a good two inches of solid wood to take these screws (see Fig. 1).

A FORT FROM A CIGAR-BOX

A splendid little fort can be made out of a cigar-box. Buy one of these deep boxes, which are sold for a penny by tobacconists, but do not pull it to pieces.

Now get some good stout cardboard and cut it up into strips about two and a half or three inches wide. This is for the " battlements " (B in Fig. 2).

Stick the battlements round the top of the box (Figs. 1 and 2).

Cigar-boxes are generally brown and forts are grey. You may paint or enamel your fort if you

like ; but there is a simple and clean way of making
both grey walls and imitation stone.

Buy a sheet of grey cartridge-paper and cut it so
that you have three strips—one for each side of the
fort. Now, with a pencil mark out the stone blocks,
as shown in the picture.

Stick the pieces of grey paper to the sides of the
fort. Do not stick the paper over the cardboard

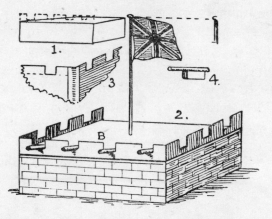

battlements ; these can be coloured grey with some
water-colour paint. Black mixed with Chinese white
makes the best grey.

The Union Jack can easily be painted on a piece
of drawing paper, and the flagstaff might be made
out of an old pen-holder, trimmed down a little.
Bore a small hole in the top of the fort for the staff.

Little cannons can be made out of wood, and if
neatly painted and glued to tiny block stands, such
" guns " look very well (Fig. 4).

A THAMES BARGE

It is quite simple to make this model of a Thames barge that will sail across a pond by itself, and there will be no troublesome carving.

Just get a flat piece of wood, eighteen inches long, five or six inches wide, and about half-inch thick, and two very thin strips about nineteen inches long and, say, two or two and a half inches wide.

The thick board is for the flat bottom of the barge,

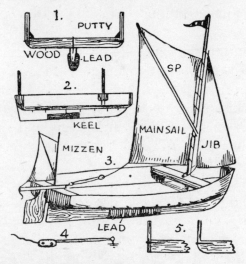

and the strips for the sides. You will want other odd bits of wood, and a long, thickish piece for the wooden keel.

Ask your grocer for one of those soft wood boxes which come from America, and you will have plenty of stout board. The thin sides should be made of very light fret-work wood, or, better still, what is called veneer wood.

Cut out your thick half-inch board roughly to the shape of the barge, as shown in Fig. 3; then make the thick back or stern-piece, and nail it on to the back (or stern) of the boat—the dark parts in Fig. 2 will show you where the thick wood comes.

Next bend your thin pieces round the sides of the barge, and tack them to the thick bottom with ordinary black pins.

Your boat's edges or " bilges " will now be sharp. If you have fastened the pins high up (Figs. 1 and 5), you can round off the " bilges " with your pocket-knife (Fig. 5).

Except for the thick piece to support the mast, your hull is now almost complete. Fig. 3 will show you how to fit the mast-step.

A thickish piece of wood about fifteen inches long and, say, one and a half inch deep will do for the wooden keel (see Fig. 2). Fasten this with panel pins or screws, driven downwards.

Get a small piece of sheet lead, turn it round the wooden keel, and tack it in place, but don't use enough lead to sink your boat if she fills.

Fix the rudder. You will steer the barge by means of her sails. Make the mast and the " sprit " (SP.) thin and light. The mast should be sixteen inches long. Tie the " sprit." It should swing freely.

Fig. 3 shows the sails. They should be of thin close stuff. The sails should never be kept in tightly when sailing. The cords, or " sheets," can be tightened or loosened if you make little blocks like that shown in Fig. 4.

AN ELASTIC-DRIVEN BOAT

A boat that will go by itself is a thing that every boy desires, and it is quite easy to make.

It is a good idea to get a box from the grocer, one with a thick end-piece such as a box in which tins of canned beef are packed. Use only one of the thick

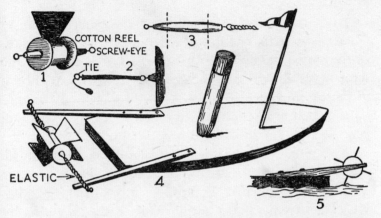

ends, which will probably be about one-half or three-quarters of an inch thick.

Cut this end-piece into the rough shape of a boat (see diagram), and be sure that your "steamer" is very wide. You can make it as large as your piece of wood will allow, but remember your boat should be at least one-third as wide as it is long.

Now cut two pieces of wood for the "horns" which project over the back or stern of your boat, and either nail or screw them on to the deck as shown (Figs. 4 and 5). On to the ends fasten some bits of wire, to which you will presently fasten the rubber strip (see Figs. 2 and 4).

For the " paddle wheel " get a very small cotton reel. Then make a plug of wood, like that shown on Fig. 3, and hammer it securely into the hole in the cotton reel. Buy two little screw-eyes and screw one of them into each end of the plug (see Fig. 3).

For the blades of the paddle cut out some bits of tin, then make holes in the reel, and put the blades in place like the one shown ready fixed in Fig. 1.

At a rubber shop buy about twopennyworth of " aeroplane strip." Do not loop it, but tie up the ends of the single pieces with thread and fasten them to the screw-eyes and to the ends of the " horns," as shown in Figs. 2 and 4.

It is better not to loop the elastic, as the boat will run for a longer time with *single* strips.

The funnel is just a cylinder of solid wood, and the mast you can add or leave out as you please.

To wind up your " engine " just turn the paddle-wheel with your hand until " black balls " form along the rubber strips, place the boat carefully in the water and release the wheel. The boat will run either backwards or forwards.

KITES

A fine tree-less stretch of ground—or a firm beach—and kite flying is hard to beat. You can easily make a kite for yourself.

Diagram A shows kites of five different types. Fig. 1 shows the highest development of the old round-headed kite, and Fig. 2 one of the popular box kites, a type from which the modern aeroplane was developed. The graceful bird kite is shown in Fig. 3, and the Malay kite, with its cambered cross-piece, in Fig. 4. This is a very simple and graceful form of kite and one which is flown by thousands of Malays on great occasions. Fig. 5 shows what is probably the simplest and most effective kite that can be

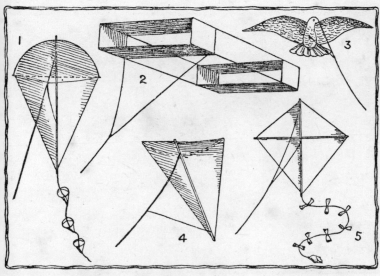

Diagram A.

devised ; it is simply a rhomboid, or double triangle, the frame of which consists merely of two light crossed sticks.

The old-fashioned round-headed kite (Fig. 1) is hard to beat, particularly if a tail is fitted with the little paper cups shown in Fig. 5, Diagram B. The method of constructing this kite is shown in Fig. 2, Diagram B. A central rod of light wood should be used, and the " bow " should be made of cane, or light tough wood. S, the stretcher, could be made of stout whipcord, or of cane. Lash the " bow " to the head of the central rod with fine water-cord, then well soak the lashing with gold size or spirit varnish. The dotted lines show how the frame should be braced with stout cord. Cover this kite with light strong paper, or, if it is a large one, with calico, which should

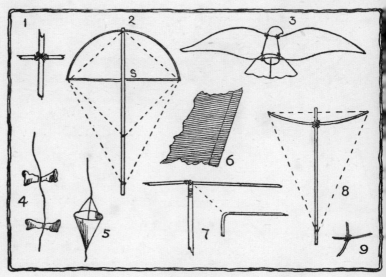

Diagram B.

be turned over and stuck together with waterproof glue (see Fig. 6, Diagram B).

The tail is not shown full length here, but a fully made up tail is sketched in Fig. 5, Diagram A. If you prefer the old-fashioned tail made up of bunches of paper, tied as shown in Fig. 4, Diagram B, use that type.

The Malay kite is shown in Fig. 4, Diagram A, and the frame in Fig. 8, Diagram B (here again the dotted lines represent string). Note how the " bow " is cambered like an aeroplane's wings ; a very thin

tough wood should be used for the frame of this kite.
In Fig. 1, Diagram B, you will see how the cross-piece
of the rhomboid kite (Fig. 5, Diagram A) is to be
lashed ; the " bow " of the Malay kite should be
lashed in the same way.

The frame of the box kite should be made of cane
or, better still, of the thin birch strip sold for model
aeroplanes. Fig. 7, Diagram B, shows a part of the
frame with the lashings (make these of thread or
water-cord). You can curve the strip in the manner
shown in Fig. 7 by first soaking the wood in water,
and then holding it over a gas jet turned down—bend
the wet wood gently, *allowing the flame to touch it.*
Paper or proofed silk may be used for making the
" planes " of the box kite.

The bird kite is very pretty, but a little tricky to
build and fly. Figs. 3 in both diagrams show the
design of this kite (the frame is given on Diagram B).
Very thin steel wire would be best for this frame,
but thin cane, lashed with thread, could be used
instead. Steel wire can be obtained at any ironmonger's ; if you use this, try lashing it with flower
wire as shown in Fig. 9, Diagram B. Unless you
make a very large bird kite paper must be used for
covering it, and it is well to remember that lightness
is of the greatest importance.

MINIATURE GARDENS

Pretty little miniature gardens are fun to make.

You will need a shallow bowl or dish, a little earth, some gravel, sand or small pebbles, tiny plants or leafy twigs that can be found in field or garden, and a little moss. Perhaps you also have some small figures that can be introduced for greater effect.

Now, having spread a protective sheet of newspaper on the floor or table, start off with an

ORIENTAL GARDEN

Fig. 1 of the diagram gives a sectional view of this to help you. Cover the bottom of your bowl or dish with a layer of clean small stones; these will supply the drainage. Fill a very small saucer with water (or you can use a piece of mirror glass) and place it in the centre of the bowl. Cover the stones and the edge of the saucer with moss. In this plant a few seedling trees.

This forms the basis of your Oriental garden and your imagination can do

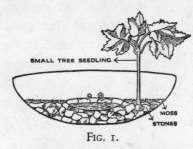

FIG. 1.

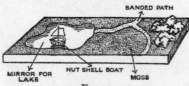

FIG. 2.

76

the rest. For instance, you can make a little bridge for the pond and perhaps a pagoda to stand beside it. One or two tiny toy swans will help the effect.

A different way of laying out this garden is shown in Fig. 2. The lid of a biscuit tin forms the foundation, and the lake is again a piece of mirror glass. The rest of the lid is covered with moss, over which wind paths of sand or fine gravel. If you make a small pile of earth or stones in one corner and cover it with moss, it will be a realistic hillock on which a small bushy plant can be placed.

You might also make a nutshell boat with a matchstick mast and a paper sail, to sail on the lake.

MARROW GARDEN

This is a novel idea for a garden and you can hang it up in a window.

You will need a small vegetable marrow and some ears of wheat or oats. Push these into the skin of the marrow, as shown in Fig. 3. Now tie a string round the marrow stalk and hang it up. There is no need to water it as the seeds will find sufficient moisture in the marrow and will soon begin to sprout.

FIG. 3.

PINE CONE GARDEN

Look for a big pine cone and keep it in a warm dry place for a day or two until it has opened out. Then stand it in the centre of a saucer, supported by damp moss. Fill the openings of the cone with fine soil and sow this with grass or canary seed. Keep the soil fairly moist and the seeds will quickly sprout.

OASIS IN THE DESERT

This garden is shown in Fig. 4. Fill a shallow bowl with sand with a scrap of mirror for a pool surrounded

FIG. 4.

by a little moss and a few stones. Make a palm tree with twigs and leaves, and set a toy camel near by.

BOX GARDEN

Here is a garden that will give plenty of scope for your imagination, for it can be arranged exactly as you would plan your ideal life-size garden.

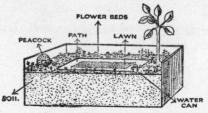

FIG. 5.

The example shown in Fig. 5 is an example of a box garden laid out in a very formal way. First of all the box, which should be of wood, is almost filled with good soil which is pushed into mounds along the sides for flower beds. A small strip of turf lies in the centre and forms a lawn, and this is surrounded by a sandy path or crazy paving made with chips of stone.

A seedling tree or two will make the garden even more attractive, and a few toy gardening tools, and perhaps a peacock with tail spread out, will give it the finishing touch.

TREES IN ORANGES

Cut a hole in the top of a large, fairly unripe orange, and scoop out all the fruit with a teaspoon. Then fill up the orange skin with a mixture of equal quantities of soil, coconut fibre, and charcoal.

Next place an acorn, or other tree seed, in this mixture and keep the soil moist. The orange skin should be kept in a light place and, as the roots begin to grow through, they should be kept cut back level with the skin. The result will be a very pretty dwarf tree.

A small lemon or orange tree can be grown in this way by planting the pip instead of an acorn. The plant should be kept in a warm room.

HOME-MADE DECORATIONS

QUITE a lot of the fun of parties and special occasions lies in decorating the rooms and tea-table beforehand. Let us take the very special occasions as they come during the year and find some jolly ways of brightening them.

EASTER

Egg Faces

This is a fine opportunity for a merry breakfast table. Offer to cook the eggs, and with a little

preparation they will cause some smiles when they reach the table.

Above are two ways of treating the eggs—and no doubt you will be able to think out plenty of other designs. Be sure to draw the faces in indelible pencil or Indian ink so that they will still be there when the eggs are boiled.

New Chicks

Save as many egg-shells as you can before Easter, and wash them. Then dot them about the table with a tiny fluffy chick (price about ½d. each) coming out of each one.

Easter Vases

This idea also needs empty egg-shells. Wash them and gum three beads to the bottom of each shell, so that it will stand alone. You can colour the shells if you like, or initial them, and place one beside each plate holding a few violets or snowdrops.

HALLOWE'EN

This festival, which falls on 31st October, is a fine excuse for a "mysterious" party, when you bob for apples in a tub of water, roast chestnuts, and pretend to tell each other's fortunes.

The ideal atmosphere to cultivate is a somewhat "witchy" one, with shaded lights, hollowed-out turnips for lanterns, curtains decorated with paper owls, black cats, and stars. You can easily make these by tracing the outlines on to paper or card and then blacking them in. If the turnip is difficult to come by, make your own lantern or lamp shade with plain paper decorated with goblins, cats, etc.

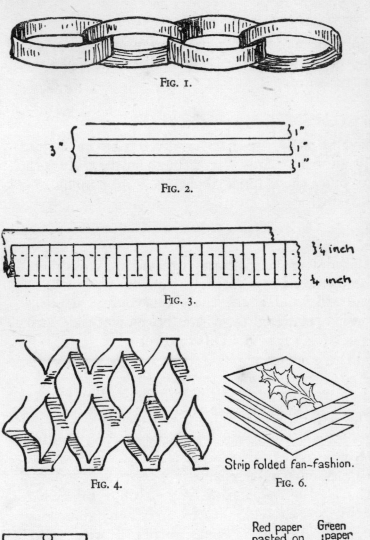

FIG. 1.

3" { }1"
}1"
}1"

FIG. 2.

} ½ inch

↓ inch

FIG. 3.

FIG. 4.

Strip folded fan-fashion.

FIG. 6.

FIG. 7.

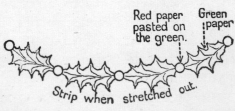

Red paper
pasted on
the green.

Green
paper

Strip when stretched out.

FIG. 8.

Fol
Fol
Fol
Fol
Fol
Fol
Fol
Fol
Fol
Fol
Fol
Fol
3 inch
Fig.

Garlands

As it takes yards and yards of chains and garlands to decorate even one room, it is as well to begin to make decorations some weeks before Christmas. In fact if you have a large cardboard box in which to keep them there is no reason why you shouldn't make garlands at any time.

For ordinary plain chains you can buy bundles of strips of paper, each about eight inches long and one inch wide, in various colours, but if you prefer it you can buy packets of crinkly paper or sheets of tissue paper, and cut strips of whatever width you like. With a light touch of paste join pieces in alternate colours to form links in the chain, as shown in Fig. 1.

A very effective chain is made by cutting tissue or crinkled paper into strips three inches wide and as long as possible. Each strip is then folded into three, lengthwise (Fig. 2). Press the folds thoroughly, then carefully cut the strips from side to side to within a quarter of an inch of each edge (Fig. 3). Unfold and pull gently, and the dainty openwork chain seen in Fig. 4 will result.

A holly festoon is a particularly " Christmassy " decoration. In this case, cut strips of green tissue paper three inches wide (Fig. 5). Fold each strip, fanwise, into square sections (Fig. 6). On the top square, draw the shape of a holly leaf, and two half berries (Fig. 7), the berries coming right up to the fold. Press the sections together tightly and cut through the folded strip over the pencilled leaf. (It will be easier to keep the papers together if paper fasteners are put over the corners). Open out carefully, and where the circles join the leaves paste small rounds of red paper for berries (Fig. 8).

Holly Hoops

One or two small toy hoops can be a great help when decorating, and look very gay if hung from the picture-rail by inexpensive red ribbon or cords. A good way to decorate them is to bind with alternate

red and green strips of tissue paper, adding a spray or two of natural or artificial holly.

Paper Balls

Jolly little balls, either self- or multi-coloured, can be hung here and there along the lengths of any sort of chain. To make the balls cut two-inch squares of tissue paper, fold into triangles, then fold again, pressing well. Partly unfold each square, take it by the centre and gently squeeze into an umbrella-like shape. Fasten a number of them together by the centres with a needle and thread until enough are joined to make a ball, leaving a long thread for attaching the ball to the chain.

A variation of this ball is to snip the edge of the folded triangle, before joining with needle and thread. Gently rub the finished ball to make it frilly.

Introducing Mr. Berry

Quaint little figures, for table decoration and for dotting about the room in place of the usual ornaments,

can be made from wire, with arms and heads of holly leaves and berries, as shown here, with bodies padded and covered with scarlet tissue paper. The legs are wire covered with scarlet paper, and you can easily draw a face on the berry-head.

Paper Table Mats

You will need some sheets of paper and a pair of scissors. Take a piece of paper (oblong or square) and fold it three times. Now clip off all four corners, and cut the three V's and the side curves shown on the upper figure on the diagram. You would hardly expect that when unfolded the paper will look like

the lower sketch (in the square), but try it and see. These two sketches were drawn round actual cuttings laid upon black paper, so that the relative sizes of the folded and unfolded pieces are correct.

This is but one of many pretty designs you can cut—try some experiments. You may cut squares, half-moonlike curves, or half-circles, and it is possible to make beautiful designs by using large pieces of paper, and folding them many times. For example, if you cut half a star on the folded paper, you will get complete stars on the finished design.

Table Novelties

When nuts and fruits are plentiful you can make all kinds of amusing novelties to decorate the party table. *Banana Boats*, or ships, can be made with the addition of matchsticks and pieces of paper, as shown. *Walnut Boats* also look attractive, especially if well displayed. The walnut is simply halved, the nut left in, and the matchstick mast stuck in, with little paper or apple-peel sails added.

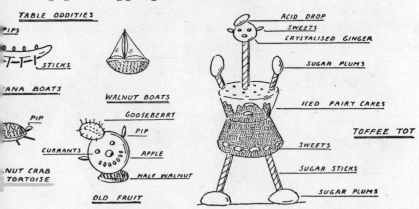

Walnut crabs and other weird animals can also be made with a few additions and a little imagination.

A row of *Phunnifaces* on the table will create great interest. You can make up " Old Fruits," " Old Beans," and " Old Things," etc., and put a " Bright Young Thing " in the centre to counterbalance all the old ones. The " Old Fruit " can be made up of various fruits on the lines suggested, the " Old Bean " can be made up of beans and pips, the " Old Thing " of any old thing, and " The Bright Young Thing " of any young thing.

Don't forget to make a *Toffee Tot* as a centre of attraction. This is made of "sugar and spice and all things nice," but it must not be eaten until all the other confections are disposed of.

Decorating Yourself

Now, while you are making so many things with nutshells and other odds and ends, try making a funny disguise for yourself with similar materials. The sketch will help you.

The *spectacles* can be made from walnut shells.

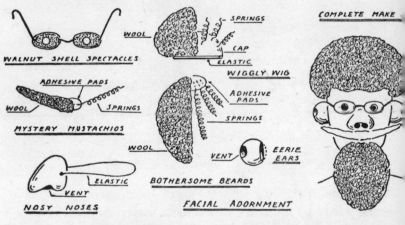

Split the nut in halves carefully, bore a hole in the centre of each section, and two small side holes, and fit together with stiff wire. For comfort the wire may be wrapped with wool. Make a number of pairs for distribution amongst your guests. The shells may be coloured with poster or oil colours, if desired, to add to the general effect.

Nosy Noses are easy to make, in any shape or colour you wish. Model the nose carefully with modelling clay, and while the clay is plastic pierce breathing vents and small holes in each side, as shown, for fixing a length of thin elastic. When the clay has set hard, colour with poster or oil colours. If you want a shiny nose, varnish when the colour is dry. Pink elastic should be used, as this will not be so easily seen.

Mystery Mustachios can be made from fine springy wire and some wool waste. Form the wire into small spiral springs by the simple procedure of winding tightly and closely around a pencil. Slip the wire off the pencil, and then cover with wool waste or cotton wool, fixing a small piece of adhesive tape at the back. This will enable the wobbly mustachio to be easily fitted to the upper lip, and it can be easily taken off. The wool may be of any suitable colour, or, if cotton wool is used, it may be previously dipped in ink.

The same idea may be applied for the making of *Bothersome Beards*. In this case quite a number of spiral springs are first prepared, and then wired or bound together at one end and fitted with a pink elastic band or adhesive tape. The wool is worked in, and left white or coloured as desired. With every movement of the face the beard will spring about in a most lively manner.

To complete the equipment in this respect make a *Wiggly Wig*. First make a skull cap of canvas or stout fabric, fix little springs all over it, and then work in the wool. You can make jet black outfits, carroty red outfits, aged white outfits, and blonde outfits, and the effect will be startling.

The making of sets of *Eerie Ears* will complete the facial adornments. A simple method is to procure some small hollow rubber balls and cut them, as shown, to fit over the ears, making a small hole in the position indicated to act as a vent, and also to allow for hearing. The crude ear-caps may then be coloured to make them more conspicuous.

Fairy for the Christmas Tree

Whatever else there is on your Christmas Tree there should be a fairy doll on the top. To dress one you will need a piece of muslin (half a yard or a yard,

according to the size of the doll), two yards of baby ribbon, about half a yard of very narrow lace, a ball of tinsel, a yard or so of wire, a small piece of net or gauze for the wings, and two silver stars. The wand is a small stick such as a skewer, covered with silver paper.

Cut out, first of all, the parts of the bodice as shown in the sketch. F is the front, the two pieces marked B are for the back, and S is a sleeve. Both, of course, will be cut alike.

Now make up the bodice by running the back pieces to the front, and hemming the back opening on each side. To make the sleeves, fold each piece along the dotted line shown, and run the edges together ; then turn the sleeve, draw in the bottom, and finish with a piece of lace. Run the sleeves into the bodice, and finish off the neck with a piece of

lace. The skirt of the fairy's frock is just a straight
piece, cut very wide to allow for fullness. Run this
together at the back, and make a deep hem round the
bottom, then turn over at the top, and run in to the

size of the doll's waist, leaving a little frill there ;
finally run the skirt on to the bodice.

The trimming is just a piece of tinsel running round
the skirt, caught up here and there with tiny bows of
baby ribbon, and a bow at the waist.

To form the wings bend pieces of thin wire, as
shown on the sketch, cover them with gauze, and
sew firmly to the back of the doll. The wand is a
tiny stick covered with silver paper, with a star pinned
to one end ; the crown is formed by twisting together
two pieces of tinsel and sewing the star to the front
of it.

BOOKBINDING IS EASY !

TO anyone who has never tackled it, bookbinding might appear to be a rather terrifyingly difficult proposition. This is not so, however, and if you study this chapter and its illustrations carefully you will no doubt feel inspired to hunt out that jealously hoarded stack of periodicals and transform some of them into neatly bound volumes, so that your favourite serial stories can be followed to the end.

Nowadays, also, a number of interesting publications are issued in the form of weekly or monthly "parts," which can be put away in a safe place until they reach completion and then bound.

You will know, if you have seen a book with its covers off, that books are built up in sections. These sections, in your case, are represented by the individual periodicals that you wish to bind. First collect them all together and neatly cut out all the pages of advertisements. Do not, of course, mutilate any page that is wanted by cutting out any small advertisements.

If the pages are fastened together with wire staples, pull these out with pliers. Then arrange the sections in their right order, with the earliest dates at the bottom, and the title page below them all. Then put the complete pile under a very heavy weight and leave, if possible, for a day or two so that the sections are pressed quite flat.

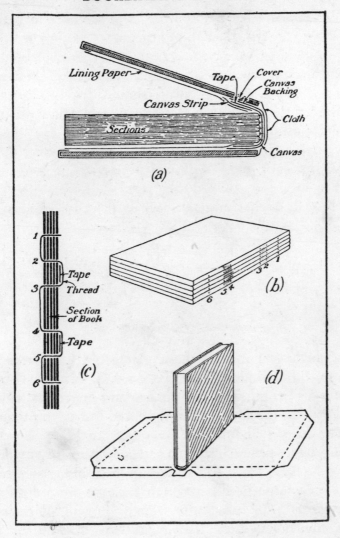

Lining Paper

Tape Cover
Canvas
Backing

Canvas Strip

Sections

Cloth

Canvas

(a)

1
2
Tape
3
Thread
Section
of Book
4
Tape
5
6
(c)

3 2 1
6 5 4
(b)

(d)

Now take two pieces of fairly wide tape, soak them
in flour paste to make them stiff and lay them out to
dry. These are to go round the sections in two places
to hold them together. While the sections are still

under pressure, rule down the back six lines in pencil as shown in Fig. *b* of the illustration, taking care that the pencil marks every section—in other words, that there are six marks on each. The spaces between lines 2 and 3, and 4 and 5, should be equal to the width of the tapes, for a reason which you will soon understand.

(*Note here.*—If the book is to be a large one, three tapes may be used with advantage ; but two will suffice for books of ordinary size.)

Instead of marking the back with pencil as already

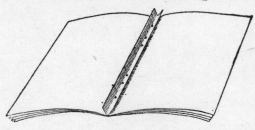

described, you may make a gauge out of a strip of tin or other thin metal. To do this, bend the strip along its length to a V shape, and make six small holes along the apex of the V, spaced just as you would space the pencil lines in the other method. To use this gauge, open each section and lay it back downwards on a board. Place the gauge upon it and pass a fine awl or a large needle through each of the holes into the paper. The sewing, in which you will, of course, use the holes thus made, will by this means be perfectly regular.

Now turn the whole pile over so that a new pile may be built up in the same order, when the sections are taken one at a time and sewn together in series.

Remove the top section, which we will call A, from the inverted pile, and, turning it over, make it the bottom one of a new pile.

Sewing

Taking a long needleful of stout thread, pass the needle with the right hand through the back of the opened-out first section at mark 1, as shown in Fig. *c*, seize the point as it comes through the inside fold (with the left hand), and pull the thread nearly through. Pass it back from left to right at point 2 ; return it through point 3, after laying it over one of the tapes. In the same way, pass the needle out at 4 and back at 5, enclosing the second tape.

The thread having been brought out at point 6, section B is laid on A, and the process of stitching repeated, but in the opposite direction, entering first at 6 and finishing at 1. The loose end of the thread is then secured by being tied tightly to the thread as it emerges from point 1.

Section C is treated similarly to A, excepting that the thread, after emerging at 6, and before entering section D, is passed through the loop between sections A and B. The process is repeated until all the sections have been sewn together and taped.

After each section is sewn, pull the thread tight, firmly but gently. Make certain that the needle has not passed through the tapes but round them, so that the tapes may be pulled tight and the sections drawn close together. When the first piece of thread is exhausted, tie another piece to it, so that the thread shall run continuously through the book. When the last section is sewn, finish off by tying the thread to the loop between the preceding pair of sections.

Gluing

Again put the pile of sections under pressure, pulling the tapes as tight as possible, after which the back is given a good serving of glue, laid on thick and worked under the tapes. While the glue is hot, lay lengthwise over the back a strip of canvas longer and two inches wider than the back, the spare at the edges being left unglued. Let the glue set hard. Then lay the book on the table, and holding it down with the left hand, tap up and down the back with a piece of wood, to round it. Do the upper half first, then turn the book over and tap the other half ; repeat this until the book has a good shape. The front edges of the book will be rather uneven, but this is un-avoidable, as it is difficult to get them level without cutting in a special machine.

Covering

The two pieces of cardboard which form the covers of the book are fastened on by **gluing** to them the projecting edges of the tapes and the free edges of the back canvas. The joint is made doubly secure by gluing two narrow strips of canvas length-wise over tape ends and back canvas (see Fig. *a*).

The boards and back are covered by a single piece of book " cloth," cut large enough to lap over the three free edges of each board (Fig. *d*) and the ends of the piece of brown paper stuck to the inside of the part which covers the back. When the cloth is dry, line the inside of the covers with stiff smooth paper.

If you are good at lettering you may like to print the title of the book on the back, or it can be written on a glued-on label.

STAMP COLLECTING

ANY one who has never collected stamps has missed a very fascinating hobby, but there is no excuse for missing it any longer, for it can be started to-day. You will soon enjoy collecting together stamps from all over the world, some printed with the most interesting pictures that, if you trace their origin, will help you tremendously with your geography and history.

How thrilling, too, to think that one day you may come across a stamp that is really valuable !

Beginner's Equipment

Now, when you first start your stamp collecting, do not be tempted to invest in a large assortment of gadgets and marvellous albums. Start with well-planned but simple equipment, and improve upon it as your collection increases.

First, the album. This should be a strong bound book which opens out quite flat, preferably with illustrations of stamps inside for your guidance. If the album on which you decide has spaces for stamps on both sides of the leaves, put sheets of tissue paper between the leaves so that the stamps do not catch on each other and get damaged.

Fixing the Stamps

Next, mounting your stamps. Never, *never* stick your stamps into the album by means of a dab of gum

or the use of stamp edging. This would mean that
if you ever wished to remove a stamp from the album
for rearrangement or examination, it would be spoilt
by the strong gum on its back and its value lessened.

The correct way to fix the stamp into the album
is by a hinge, and hinges can be bought very cheaply
from any stamp dealer. Each hinge is a small piece
of thin paper, gummed on one side only, which is
folded in two, one end being fixed to the stamp, the

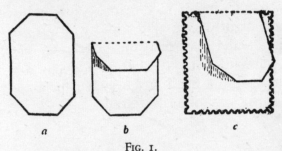

a   *b*   *c*

FIG. 1.

Stamp hinge: (a) *flat;* (b) *folded;* (c) *on the stamp.*

other to the page, so that the stamp is actually
" hinged."

To use the hinge, place it gummed side downwards
on a piece of paper. Turn over not more than a
quarter of an inch of the upper end, as shown in Fig. *b*
of the illustration ; moisten the turned-over portion ;
hold the hinge down and with tweezers place the
stamp on the moistened part, so that the hinge is
midway across and the crease in the paper just shows
beyond the extreme upper edge, and press it down
with a piece of blotting-paper. The stamp is now on
the hinge (Fig. *c*), ready for mounting in its proper
place by the obvious method of moistening the longer

end of the hinge and fixing it on the page. The best way of doing this is by dabbing the tip of your little finger on your tongue and then applying it to the hinge.

A good idea is to fix a permanent " buffer " on each stamp, so that any possible wear or tear from removal of hinges is done away with.

To do this, get some very thin, tough grease-proof paper, gummed on one side and highly glazed on the other. Cut it into small strips a quarter of an inch wide and slightly longer than the width of the hinges. Fix this " buffer " strip to the upper part of the back of the stamp, so that its outside edge is exactly level with the extreme top. Then attach the hinge to this buffer in the way described above.

Tweezers

Tweezers, mentioned earlier, are very important things to include in your stamp-collecting outfit. If you constantly handle the stamps with your fingers they will soon become soiled, no matter how clean you know your hands to be. The natural moisture on your hands will leave marks which, though at first invisible, will soon begin to show.

For this reason use tweezers. There is not the slightest difficulty with them, and after a while you will prefer them to your fingers. If and when a finger must be brought into contact with a stamp, especially unused or lightly postmarked, interpose a scrap of tissue paper or, better still, wear a very thin indiarubber " stall " on the particular finger. This may seem " finicky," but the difference in value between two copies of a rare stamp, one of which differs from the other only in that it has a finger-mark, is very great.

There are several kinds of tweezers on the market, two of which are shown here, but preference may be

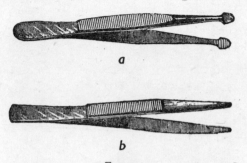

a

b

Fig. 2.

Tweezers: (a) *rounded ends;* (b) *pointed ends.*

given to those with curved ends, the extremities being rounded and very slightly roughened on the inner surface. The outside parts, where the fingers grasp them, should be well milled to give a firm hold. In use it is more convenient to keep the concave side of the curved ends uppermost.

Perforations

Now we come to perforation gauges. Perforations are holes punched out of the paper between the stamps on the sheets, as sold at the post office, to make separation easy. These holes are classified according to gauge—that is, the number to be found in a certain agreed space.

Many years ago a Frenchman, Dr. Legrand, propounded the idea of differentiating the various gauges

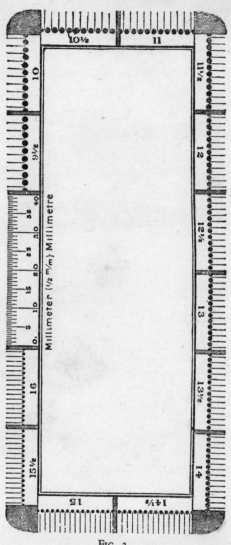

Fig. 3.

Perforation gauge.

by counting the number of holes in the space of two
centimetres, the decimal system naturally being selected.

A chart showing the various numbers of holes within this space is termed a perforation gauge, and a typical specimen is shown on page 102.

Choose a gauge which is printed on stiff card. The various rows of round dots corresponding to the perforation holes should be arranged round the edge of the card, and each dot should be dissected with a fine line at right angles to the row. This card may usefully include a four-centimetre scale divided accurately into millimetres, which should be subdivided into quarters; also a two-inch scale, similarly subdivided.

To use the gauge, place the stamp so that the side which you wish to " measure " will be alongside a row of dots, the first dot being exactly coincident with the first perforation hole. When you have found a row of dots, all of which coincide with all the holes, the figures placed against that particular row will indicate the gauge of perforation on that side of the stamp.

In recording the perforation of stamps, a certain system is adopted, as follows—the gauges now given being, of course, arbitrary: (a) if the perforation gauges the same all round the stamp, it is " perf. 14 "; (b) if the top and bottom are of one gauge, and the sides of another, it is " perf. $14 \times 12\frac{1}{2}$," the horizontal being taken first; (c) if, as may happen, each side is of a different gauge, the order is top, right, bottom, left, say, " perf. $14 \times 13 \times 12 \times 15$."

Watermarks

All the stamps of Great Britain, most of those of the British Colonies, and a small proportion of those of foreign countries, are printed on paper which, when held up to the light, shows some device appearing more transparent than the surrounding portions.

This is termed a watermark, and is one of the chief protections against forgery though, as a rule, it cannot be seen when the stamp is on a letter.

When you have been collecting stamps for a while you will appreciate the fact that it is not always easy to tell whether a stamp is or is not watermarked ; and, as the absence or presence of a watermark may mean

Fig. 4.
Watermark detector.

a great difference in value a " detector " has been devised.

The watermark-detector shown here consists of a small square dish of black porcelain or marble, having a recessed portion. If the stamp with the elusive watermark is placed face downwards in this recess and benzine is poured over it, the watermark, if it exists, will most probably show up quite plainly.

The benzine, which should be of the best quality, will not harm the stamp ; but, as it is very inflammable, it should not be used in a room where there is a naked light or a fire.

Catalogue

A stamp catalogue is not absolutely essential if you have a well-illustrated album, but it is certainly very useful. It will help you to identify your stamps and guide you in many other ways.

Some General Hints

Now that you have all the essential equipment all that you have to do is collect some stamps ! Friends and relations will no doubt be glad to pass on stamps from their foreign correspondence, and you can also buy quite cheaply packets of assorted stamps from any stamp dealer.

Sometimes the value of rare stamps is increased by leaving them on the original envelope, but most of them will require to be removed. Do not soak them in water to do this. The proper way is to lay the envelope, face upwards, on wet blotting-paper until the envelope is thoroughly wetted ; then the stamp may be easily peeled off. Do not put salt in the water used for the blotting-paper in the hope of stabilizing the colours of the stamp. Never trim stamps unless their edges are very irregular.

HOW TO DRAW

MOST people like to draw—even if it is only aimless " doodling " while they are answering the telephone or thinking out some problem. They may not do it very well, but there is no reason why you should not improve your drawing so that you can spend many happy hours with pen, pencil, or brush.

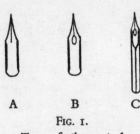

A   B   C

Fig. 1.

Types of nibs required.

For pencil drawing you require a range of fairly soft pencils. If you are going to use a pen, buy yourself a set of nibs as shown here in Fig. 1. That shown at A is made from extremely fine and flexible steel, and will produce lines of every possible gradation of thickness. It should not be used, however, until some degree of proficiency has been attained ; for in unpractised hands its fineness may lead to splaying the point.

For practical purposes the nib shown at B will be found the most useful. The old-fashioned steel crow quill illustrated at C is still favoured by many artists. You will soon discover which nib suits your own particular style of drawing.

Now for your brushes. You will want three sable-hair brushes, sizes Nos. 3, 5, and 7. Also one or two flat hog's-hair brushes, such as are used for oil-painting. These will be found extremely useful for "body-colour" work, which you will read about farther on in this chapter. Preference should be given to short-haired brushes similar to that shown at A in Fig. 2. Should these not be obtainable, get brushes like that shown at B, and cut down the hairs at the point in-dicated by the dotted line.

Having laid in your stock of pens and pen-cils, acquire a piece of soft rubber, some drawing-pins, a draw-ing-board, a supply of paper or card, and some Conte crayon and car-bon chalks, which can all be bought at any artists' colourman. You will also need some ink and Chinese white.

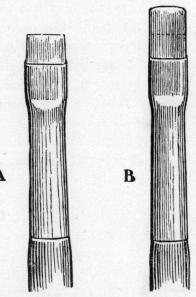

FIG. 2.
Hog's-hair brushes.

The most satisfactory ink is that known as "Waterproof." It is better than ordinary Indian ink as it never clogs the pen nor results in "missing" lines. Chinese white can be bought in tubes or bottles.

Wash drawing will be mentioned later on, and for this you will require some black. Lamp-black is the most favoured as, by working in a little gamboge, a certain warmth of tone can be obtained.

GETTING TO WORK

Now pin a sheet of paper to your drawing-board and get to work. Practise first at drawing people. As a start try to get your proportions right. Remember that a person's head is about one-seventh of his total height ; that his hips occur at a point half-way ; that his fingertips reach half-way down his thigh ; that his elbows are level with the top of his hips.

To arrive at the ideal proportions of a face in profile draw four horizontal parallel lines each one inch apart. A gently sloping line joining the top two represents the forehead. Another line, sloping at the same angle but beginning slightly in from the first, joins the second and third lines for the nose. The next line, joining the third and fourth lines and sloping slightly backwards from the nose, gives you the mouth and chin. Draw a curving line from the top of the forehead for the crown and back of the head ; then add an eye in profile on the second line down and also a mouth just beneath the third line. The ear will be the same length as the nose, between the second and third lines, and a curved line from the chin forms the jawline coming to meet the ear.

Practise drawing hands and feet, too. It is a good idea to carry a small sketchbook around in your pocket to jot down small details that you may notice when you are out among people. Make a point of " collecting " an assortment of expressions in your book ; most expression depends on eye and mouth, and you should practise drawing both in profile and full view. If you like drawing humorous sketches, study the illustrations given here in Figs. 3 to 6, for they show how features can be slightly exaggerated to give a funny effect.

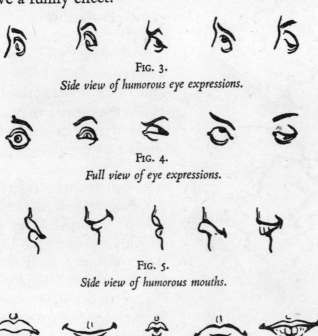

FIG. 3.

Side view of humorous eye expressions.

FIG. 4.

Full view of eye expressions.

FIG. 5.

Side view of humorous mouths.

FIG. 6.

Full view of humorous mouths.

In fact, most successful drawing depends on the artist's powers of observation and memory. Cultivate the habit of noticing how various actions are performed and the way different implements are held.

CARICATURING

This is quite a definite style of drawing, examples of which you can see in any newspaper nowadays.

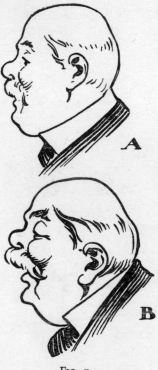

A

B

FIG. 7.
An example of exaggeration.

In a caricature, although a good likeness to the person drawn is always present, some peculiarity or mannerism is exaggerated.

All your subject's idiosyncrasies should be noted and then accentuated on paper, the entire face or figure being drawn in with as few strokes as possible. At first only heads should be attempted, and a good photograph is the best model from which to copy. The point which is to form the base of the caricature should then be studied most carefully and exaggerated only to such an extent that no part of the original likeness is marred or destroyed.

Fig. 7 shown here depicts features A which can be exaggerated as shown in the caricature B.

SHADING

Although simple outline drawings are most suitable for some purposes, sometimes you will want to add what is known as " colour." This does not mean that you will need your box of paints. " Colour " in black and white drawing is supplied by various methods of shading.

An example of this is given in Figs. 8 and 9,
together with two types of shading (Fig. 10). If you

FIG. 8.
This sketch lacks "colour."

FIG. 9.
"Colour" has been added.

wish for something heavier, why not try an all-over
shading first of thin black lines, with the folds and
shadowed parts of the subject in solid black?

WASH DRAWING

This is done with a brush and may be divided
into three main sections: pure wash, by which is
meant all the different tones and effects obtained by a

greater or less amount of water being mixed with the black ; body colour, by which is understood the mixing of black and Chinese white to form the various tones ; thirdly, a combination of the previous two.

In the last-mentioned, chalk and pure colour may be utilized for the working out of the design, the finishing touches being put in with body colour. From this last method the most satisfactory results may be obtained.

Pure wash : One method is to outline the sketch

Fig. 10.
Two kinds of shading.

in pencil, putting in the shadows with pure wash, deep black or, according to the requirements, softening the edges of the shadows and then taking a wash over the whole. In this case the detail is put in afterwards. High lights can be added when the drawing is otherwise complete. The use of Chinese white for high lights is occasionally supplemented by scratching with a penknife.

Body colour : To start, take a quantity of black and Chinese white upon the palette ; the combination should be a shade darker than you require, as it dries lighter on the card. The different tones should be worked in quickly while the mixture is wet. When once the colour has dried upon the board, never disturb it ; but should the result not be a success, wipe off the faulty part with a sponge or soft rag and repaint the portion.

Combination working : Mix in a saucer enough black and white to form a light grey ; add a little gum arabic and stir well. Only sufficient gum should be used to ensure the composition being slightly sticky. Now take a sponge and, dipping it into the mixture, smear it evenly over the cardboard intended for the drawing. When the coat is dry the drawing should be made upon it in black chalk.

Next work with either pure or body-colour, but instead of adding lights, procure them by damping the parts to be lightened with the point of the brush and wiping the composition away swiftly with a soft rag.

DECORATIVE WORK

You may, at some time or other, wish to design a cover for a book, or perhaps draw a decorative illustration for a magazine. The drawings in Fig. 11 show you how flowers and twigs may be made conventionally decorative.

Diagram A in Fig. 12 shows a more elaborate form of the scroll B.

Lettering always looks most attractive on a ribbon and you are shown in Fig. 13 how to draw the ribbon most realistically. Secure a length of tape to the table or drawing board with pins, as shown in the illustration, and there is your model.

An easy way of drawing foliage is to take the ink or colour on to a brush and hold it at right angles to

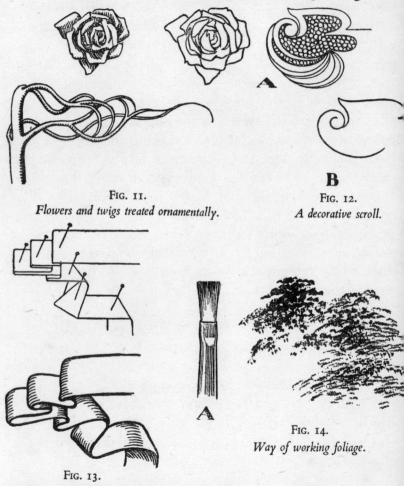

FIG. 11.
Flowers and twigs treated ornamentally.

B

FIG. 12.
A decorative scroll.

A

FIG. 14.
Way of working foliage.

FIG. 13.
Working a ribbon for a heading.

the card, dab it on as required. Figs. 14 and 15 illustrate the brush used for different types of foliage and the result obtained.

For grass, as shown in Fig. 16, a flat hog's-hair or sable brush has been greatly splayed out and cut away.

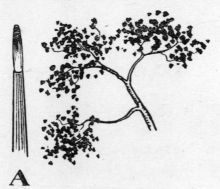

FIG. 15.
Adding leaves to branches.

FIG. 16.
Grass-work done with brush.

By taking the end of the brush dipped in the ink, and passing it lightly over the surface of the board, the effect of grass will be given.

LEATHER WORK

WHENEVER Christmas or birthdays come round one usually thinks how nice it would be to be able to make interesting presents at home, and leather-work can solve quite a number of problems in this direction.

Perhaps you have never experimented with leather work and do not know quite how to set about it, but you will find that it is fairly easy when once you have started.

HOW TO BEGIN

Let us begin with the materials. Different kinds of leather are used for different purposes, the varieties most commonly used being chamois, suede, doeskin, calf, skiver, and velvet Persian.

Chamois, thin suede, and doeskin are used for gloves ; and skiver, a thin leather, is used for lining. As this chapter is intended mainly for beginners we will deal with velvet Persian, which is perhaps the most generally useful of all as it is suitable for all kinds of articles—handbags, card and note cases, hats and hat trimmings, belts, blotters, book-carriers, etc. It is a soft, but strong, suede-like leather of moderate price, and it can be had in many beautiful shades.

YOUR TOOLS

These need not cost very much for simple work. They should consist of :

1. A punch. This is a tool for making holes in the leather so as to enable one to join two pieces together by a thong.

There are two kinds of punch to be had—one that

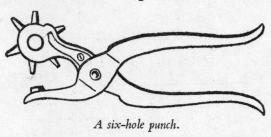

A six-hole punch.

is driven through the leather by a hammer, and one that is worked like a pair of pincers. The hammer-driven punch is the cheaper, but the other is much quicker and less laborious to use, and makes a very neat hole, so on all accounts it is to be recommended. It can be obtained in varying sizes according to the dimensions of the hole required ; one make has a revolving disc which is supplied with six different punches all of different size, and by turning the disc the worker can get exactly the hole required. This six-hole punch, shown in the illustration, is more expensive than a one-hole punch, but it is worth getting if you are going to do leather work of different kinds.

2. A board, upon which to cut the leather. It should be strong, with a smooth surface. A drawing-

board or pastry board or smooth-topped deal table would be quite suitable, or a slab of slate or marble is good.

3. A knife. Special leather knives are sold, but a sharp pocket knife will serve very well. Some workers use a very sharp pair of scissors ; although this method is not recommended, it is possible to get quite good results with scissors.

SETTING TO WORK

Leather is sold by the square foot *outside* measurement. This means that all jagged ends and rough edges are included in the measurement, so that when buying a skin of, say, five square feet you must not count on getting this amount in regular unbroken surface. In fact, it is quite possible that you may not get more than twenty-one inches by eighteen inches in good, unflawed square. On the other hand, every scrap of the jagged strips and ends can be used ; there need not be a square inch of waste in the whole skin. Even the tiny round pieces that are stamped out by the punch can be kept for decorative purposes.

Cutting : The pattern of every article made should be first cut out in paper ; the paper pattern should then be laid on the skin and the outline carefully traced on the leather in pencil. If you are going to do your cutting with a knife, spread the leather out flat on the board, using your knife nearly upright, with its blade pressed firmly against the side of a ruler as a guide for the straight parts, and cut slowly with a firm and steady pressure. When cutting corners, a square or a metal triangle is a great help in keeping them absolutely true.

Punching : It is a good idea to place a small piece of cardboard or a scrap of thick leather between the jaws of the punch, underneath where the hole is to be. This has a double advantage : it prevents your leather coming into contact with the hard surface beneath the punch, and it also keeps the punch itself from getting blunt as soon as it otherwise would. Further, if your punch is not as sharp as it ought to be, it prevents it from tearing the skin, and enables it to stamp a clean, sharply cut hole.

When punching holes for lacing two pieces of leather together you must judge what distance apart to stamp the holes, according to the size and character of the article you are making ; a very useful lacing is one in which the holes are about quarter-inch apart and about quarter-inch from the edge of the leather.

Joining : The thong should be just wide enough to go easily through the holes, and should be pointed at the end for easy threading. If possible, have the thong long enough to do the whole of the lacing without a join, for a join tends to spoil the appearance and takes from the strength of the lacing. If, however, a join is unavoidable, either sew the two pieces of the thong together beforehand, arranging the join in a position on the wrong side of the work ; or, when the first piece of thong is nearly used up, seccotine the under side of it when pulling it through the last two holes, pressing it down firmly into position : then start the new thong over this seccotined piece of the old one, treating it in the same way.

Thonging is usually done in overcasting stitch, but it may be varied when making a flat join by using two thongs at the same time and lacing in the form of a cross. These two methods are illustrated here.

Instead of thonging, you may join two pieces of leather by sewing them, either by hand or machine.

Thonging in overcasting stitch.

A flat join; the thongs laced to form a cross.

In making gloves the skins must be sewn together, of course, not laced. Hand-sewn gloves are put together with what is called up-and-down stitch. This is only ordinary running stitch, but each stitch must be taken singly, making sure that each stitch and each space is of even length.

Joining by machine-sewn seams is only suitable if the leather is fairly thin : bags, hats, stationery-cases often have the seams machine-sewn. To flatten a machine-sewn seam hold a moderately hot iron bottom upwards, open out the seam turnings and lightly draw across the iron. If you can, try to find some one to help you do this, so that one of you holds the iron while the other draws the seams across it.

TO MAKE A SHOPPING BAG

Material required : Two pieces of velvet Persian, each about eleven inches by twelve inches for the

back and front of the bag. A long narrow piece
about one and a quarter inches wide for the gusset,
and equal in length to once the breadth of the bag
and twice the depth ; narrow strips quarter-inch wide
for the thongs.

Punch holes all round the two big pieces of leather,

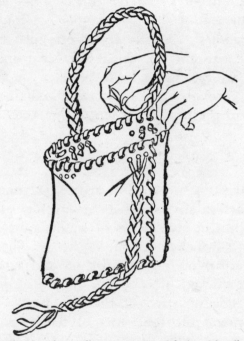

Shopping-bag ; showing insertion of plaited handle.

taking care that the holes in both pieces correspond
exactly in position. To ensure this, punch through
both thicknesses of leather at the same time, if possible ;
if not, punch the second set of holes through the first.
Now punch holes along each side of the gusset, again
taking care that these holes come exactly opposite

those in the front and back of the bag. Lace the gusset to the sides of the bag, by overcasting with a quarter-inch thong, putting two stitches into each corner hole. Overcast all round the top of the bag to give an ornamental finish.

For the handles make two plaits of three thongs, from eight inches to twelve inches long, as desired. Punch four sets of three holes (one set for each end of both handles), each set about one inch below the top of the bag and the same distance from the side gusset. Pass each strand of the plait at both ends separately through these holes, and knot the ends on the inside of the bag, as shown in the sketch.

NOW FOR A WRITING CASE

To make this most useful article, cut one piece of leather nineteen and a half inches by nine inches (for the cover). Cut two pieces of leather nine inches by five and a half inches (for the pockets). Then cut one piece of leather eight inches by six and a half inches (for centre pocket). Scoop out a curve in one of the nine-inch sides in each of the side pockets. Punch holes all round the four sides of the cover, and the three unscooped sides of the side pockets, taking care that the holes in the cover and the pockets correspond exactly in position. (See instructions on this point in directions for making a shopping bag.)

Place the centre pocket in position, exactly in the middle between the two side pockets, with its base level with the base of the cover. Punch holes along the base of this centre pocket to correspond with the holes in the base of the cover. Also, punch holes down the two eight-inch sides of the centre pocket—that is, along the lines marked FG, XY, in the diagram. If any difficulty is found in reaching the lines FG, XY, with the punch, fold one end of the cover into a neat roll, as shown, and slip between the jaws of the punch.

Now lay the cover face downwards on the table and place all three pockets in position face upwards.

Using a quarter-inch thong, lace with overcasting

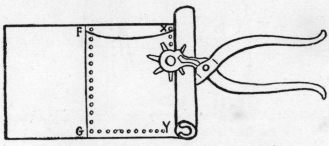

Writing-case; holes being punched for centre pocket.

stitch all round the four sides of the cover ; lacing, of course, through both thicknesses of leather when you come to where the pockets are placed in position. Lace the sides of the centre pocket to the cover with an up-and-down stitch.

The case is now complete, but if machining presents no difficulty, it greatly adds to the strength to run a row of machining all round the edge about quarter of an inch inside the lacing. The sides of the centre pocket may be machine-sewn to the cover instead of being laced.

The two side pockets are for holding letters, envelopes, etc., the centre pocket being for the correspondence block, the cardboard back of which is slipped into it. If the back of the block is too wide for the pocket, it may be cut to fit.

When the case is closed the two side pockets lie

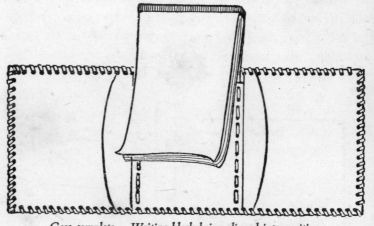

Case complete.   Writing block being slipped into position.

one over the other across the centre, the cardboard back of the block keeping the case in shape.

Card cases, treasury-note cases, handkerchief cases, and many other articles can be made of square or oblong pieces of leather, cut, folded, and thonged to suit the special requirements ; but in making anything in which success depends greatly on shape and measurement, such as hats, slippers, gloves, etc., a good paper pattern should be made, and tested, before cutting into the leather.

PRESS STUDS

Many leather articles need to be finished off with a fastening. Press studs, of a particular make, suitable for leather work, should be used for this. You can, if you wish, buy a special tool for putting in the press studs, but it can be done easily with an ordinary hammer.

Each stud consists of four parts as shown here—A, B, C, D. A and B together form the under half of the stud; C and D together form the upper half. To insert the stud, proceed as follows:

1. Punch a hole in the leather where the under half of the stud is to go; and, in a corresponding position in the overlying flap, punch another hole for the upper half.

2. Cut two small rounds of leather equal in size

A   B   C   D

The four parts of a press stud fastening.

to the bases of A and C, and punch a hole in the middle of each round. Put these rounds on to A and C, fitting them over the necks of the little projections.

3. Insert A (from underneath) in the hole that was punched for the lower half of the stud, and place B on top of it. Insert C (from underneath) in the hole that was punched in the flap, and place D on top of it.

4. Place all four parts in position (*i.e.* one above the other), exactly, and, putting bits of old leather above D and under A to prevent the article from being marked, give one or two sharp knocks with the hammer on D. This blow will spread the little projections of the stud enough to make them catch, and will thus put the stud into working order.

5. To open for the first time, insert the blade of the scissors between the upper and lower halves of the stud. If B should come away from A when the stud is opened, replace as before and hammer again.

INTERESTING THINGS TO KNOW

THE pictures on this and the following pages contain information that you are sure to find useful at some time.

USEFUL KNOTS AND HOW TO TIE THEM

The pictures on this and the following page show some useful knots, hitches, etc. The end of a rope is

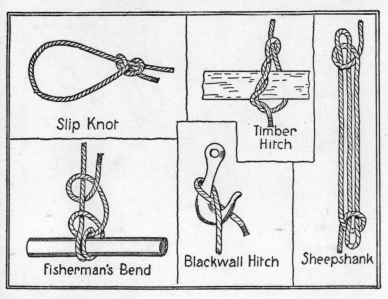

Slip Knot

Timber Hitch

Fisherman's Bend

Blackwall Hitch

Sheepshank

indicated by a dark " serving " of twine ; the ragged end indicates where the main, or " standing," part of the rope is broken away for illustrative purposes.

The Reef Knot, Full Reef Knot, the Carrick Bend, the Fisherman's Knot, and the Sheet Bend are used

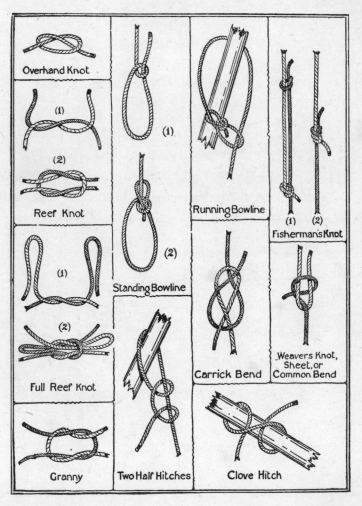

for fastening two ropes, etc., together. The Fisherman's Knot is a favourite with anglers for tying gut. In making the Sheet Bend, loop the end of one rope, and pass the end of the other through and round the loop, and between the loop and its own " standing " part.

The Standing Bowline, much used by sailors, gives a loop which will not slip under strain. The Running Bowline is a good self-tightener. The Two Half Hitches and the Clove Hitch are simple methods of attaching a rope to an object without the use of a knot. The two turns of the Clove Hitch are brought close together after being formed as shown in the illustration.

The Fisherman's Bend is useful for securing a rope to an anchor ring or bucket handle ; the Timber Hitch is used for lifting logs and other heavy objects. The Blackwall Hitch makes a loaded rope fast to a hook, and the Sheepshank shortens a long rope.

SIGNALLING

The two codes given on pages 130, 131, and 132 can be very helpful—especially the Morse, which can be tapped, flashed with a torch, and even written. The semaphore alphabet is familiar to all Scouts and Guides and is widely used by sailors.

THE MORSE CODE

This code consists of dots and dashes, which are usually tapped out on a " buzzer." The dots are indicated by a tap followed by only a short interval. A longer interval follows the dashes. Of course, if you are using a torch to flash your message, you simply use short flashes and long flashes.

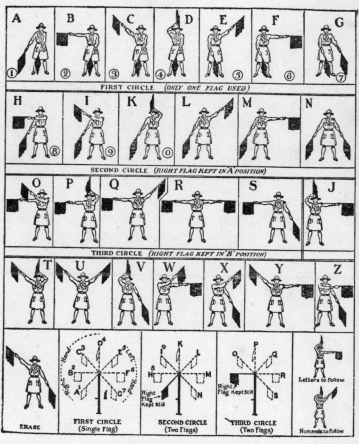

The Semaphore Alphabet.

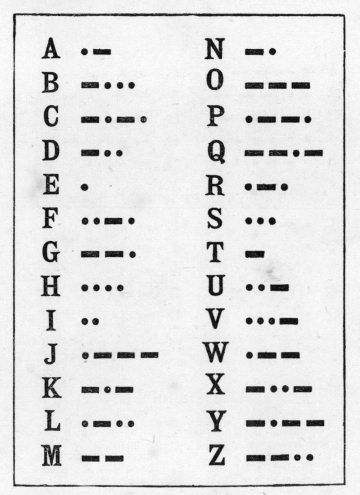

The Morse Alphabet.

FIGURES IN MORSE

These extra signs will help you to frame your messages.

FIGURES

1 • — — — —		**6** — • • • •
2 • • — — —		**7** — — • • •
3 • • • — —		**8** — — — • •
4 • • • • —		**9** — — — — •
5 • • • • •		**0** — — — — —

ABBREVIATED FIGURES (Continental)

1 • —		**6** — • • • •
2 • • —		**7** — • • •
3 • • • —		**8** — • •
4 • • • • —		**9** — •
5 •		**0** —

When the Abbreviated Figures are used, they must be preceded by the sign **FI** (Figures Intended) and followed by the sign **FF** (Figures Finished).

OTHER SIGNS

Get ready. A succession of dots continued till acknowledged (or **VE**)

End of message, **VE** or **AR**
Repeat, **IMI**
Word after, **WA**
Message received, **R**
Move to your right, **MR**
Move higher up, **MH**

Full stop, **AAA**
Erase, 8 dots (or **IMI**)
Word before, **WB**
Danger, **SOS**
Move to your left, **ML**
Move lower down, **MO**

Notes.—The dot is called "Iddy" and the dash "Umpty." To prevent confusion in dictating, some letters are named as follows : **A**, Ack ; **B**, Beer ; **D**, Don ; **M**, Emma ; **P**, Pip ; **S**, Esses ; **T**, Tock ; **V**, Vick.

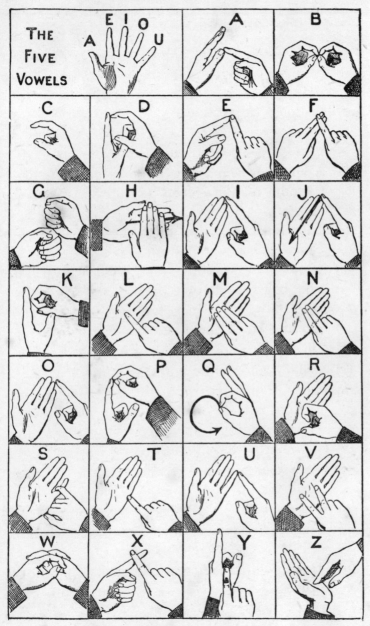

Letters are formed with hands and fingers.

THE RIGHT WAY TO TACKLE IT

As one's elders are so apt to tell one, there is a right and a wrong way of doing everything. Study the pictures on the next page and surprise everyone by doing things properly the very first time !

(a) Open a step-ladder fully before mounting it, and avoid crashing to the floor.

(b) A Union Jack must have the broad white stripe of the diagonal cross (x) upwards near the pole.

(c) To ventilate a room, open the sash at the top as well as at the bottom.

(d) Stand a wet umbrella handle downwards to drain. If it is a silk one, open it, and stand it on its handle.

(e) Spread a wet cycle cape over a chair to dry.

(f) Climb over a locked gate at the hinged end.

(g) Stand a gun or rifle with the barrel vertical.

(h) Pull up your trousers to the top of your boots before putting on cycle clips. This prevents them bagging at the knees.

(k) How a heavy box should be carried upstairs.

(l) On a windy day face the wind to open an umbrella.

(m) When opening a bottle of ink or other liquid that may damage your clothes, turn the neck of the bottle away from you.

(n) How to help a cart that has stuck in mud or a rut.

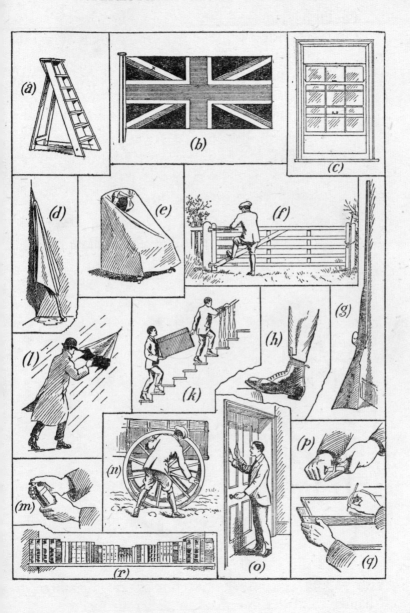

(o) Push a jammed door at the point where it sticks.

(p) When using a knife, make the strokes outwards, away from you.

(q) When accurate ruling has to be done, place the pencil point on the exact spot through which the line has to be drawn, and move the ruler or square up to it.

(r) Put heavy books at the ends of the bookshelf.

POINTS OF A HORSE

Perhaps you expected the coronet of a horse to be on his head? This picture will enlighten you!

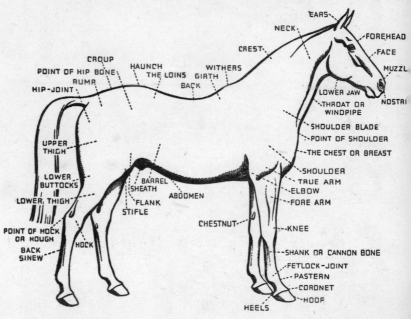

You should remember that horses are measured in "hands," and that one hand equals four inches.

A HORSE'S EQUIPMENT

The bridle is put on first, when you are standing sideways with the horse on your right.

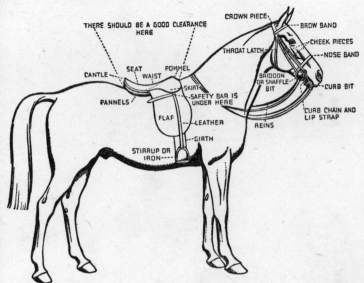

The horse is saddled from the off or right-hand side, as the girth is left fastened on that side.

PART II
YOUR PETS

(240)

10

EMERGENCY FEEDING

In war-time it may not be possible for your pets to have the same foods as in normal times. Where there are official regulations regarding this, as in the case of oats for rabbits, your seed merchant will be able to tell you what to do to obtain foodstuffs; and with regard to substitute foods for cats, dogs, and birds your local animal welfare society will give you good advice.

DOGS

THERE is no other pet whose companionship, faithfulness, and capacity for fun are so great as a dog's. If you are going to have a dog and have never had one before, you must make sure that you

Fox terrier.

know how to house him and look after him properly.

If you are going to keep a small toy dog he will be able to live indoors, and will require only a box large enough for him to lie down comfortably, and raised about one foot from the floor. Two pieces of warm carpet will do for bedding.

MAKING A KENNEL

A larger dog should live outside the house and will require a kennel. This can be bought, or you might try your hand at making one yourself—but be sure that it is draught- and weather-proof.

The kennel should be made of half-inch boarding with a width of eighteen inches, a depth of thirty inches, and a height of twenty-four inches ; this should be suitable for a medium-sized dog. Let it rest above ground on two pieces of wood, as shown in Fig. 1.

FIG. 1.
A simple kennel.

Make the roof overlapping and sloping to carry off rain, and cut a hole about one foot wide in the side or front for your dog to go in and out.

It is a good idea, too, to make a covered run to your dog's house. Put together a stout frame, so as to enclose the house in a width of at least three or four feet. Fasten to it some strong wire-netting (see Fig. 2), covered in with a sloping wood roof and containing a door. Before starting to make this kennel choose a dry, sheltered spot, and measure off exactly the space you intend devoting to it.

Several coats of paint should be given to preserve

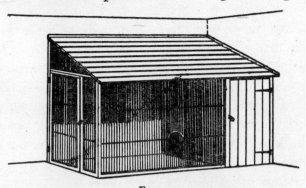

FIG. 2.
Covered run attached to a kennel.

the woodwork, and it is a good plan to cover the roof with special rainproof roofing felt.

A good supply of clean straw, changed as often as possible, forms the best bedding for the dog kept outdoors.

EXERCISE

Dogs need plenty of exercise. Only a watch-dog should be chained, and even he should be exercised regularly ; the ordinary dog ought to have plenty of freedom. The morning is a good time for the dog to have his necessary exercise in the form of a run ; he will then enjoy a spell of freedom to the full. Late in the evening, before sleep, he will keep fit if he has a little more exercise.

Never make your dog run about after a meal. He will be glad to rest at that time.

FEEDING DOGS

Some dogs thrive well on only one meal a day, but most prefer two meals.

In the morning, give your dog a breakfast of dog biscuits. The next meal should be in the evening, when he can have some more biscuit, over which gravy has been poured, or a portion of bread and meat. To keep him healthy, he should be given every other day a supply of greens cooked and chopped up.

The leavings from the dinner table can be given to your dog, but a word of warning is necessary. Such scraps often consist of fat, and too much greasy matter is not advisable. Nor should you put into his feeding-dish any fish bones or small bones from game that are easily swallowed, or are likely to stick in his throat. He will thoroughly enjoy gnawing a big bone.

Supply a dish of fresh water every day.

CLEANLINESS

Keep your dog scrupulously clean. His coat should be bright and glossy, his eyes sparkling, and his muzzle and paws without a dirty stain. Use the brush and comb often ; long-haired dogs, especially, need grooming every day.

Most short-haired dogs need a bath every fortnight. Use for this an old zinc bath, warm water, dog soap, and a brush. Rinse well and dry him thoroughly afterwards. In cold weather a dry shampoo is to be preferred. Long-haired dogs should not be washed so frequently.

CATS

THE cat, that warm, cuddly, and yet most dignified creature, is often sorely misunderstood !

Many people appear to think that a cat can live happily on any odd scraps from the table and an occasional saucer of milk, mak-  ing up the balance of her diet with a neatly caught mouse.

Your cat should be looked after as carefully as your dog, fed adequately and at regular times.

In addition to milk, give your cat at least two good meals a day. Table scraps, including bits of meat, gravy, and a small amount of green vegetables, will usually be sufficient. Bread and milk in the morning, scraps left from the midday meal of the household, and another meal of scraps at night will be sufficient, while kittens require more frequent feeding.

Cats should always have access to grass, which they eat with relish, as this is good for them medicin- ally. If you have no garden, grow some grass in a box. Put down fresh drinking water for your cat every day, as milk is not sufficient to quench her thirst.

HOUSE TRAINING

A cat can easily be trained in habits of cleanliness, but the training must begin from kittenhood. When a cat is kept in a house where there is no garden, it should always be provided with a good-sized tin tray covered with earth ; the earth, of course, should be changed frequently.

YOUR CAT'S COAT

Cats are most particular about their toilette, and pussy will keep herself scrupulously clean so long as you keep her in good health.

Long-haired cats should have their coats combed regularly with a special comb, otherwise when they wash themselves they are apt to swallow loose hairs.

KITTENS

When a mother cat has kittens she should be given a warmly lined box or basket in a quiet, draught-proof place and left quite alone. If you disturb her she may harm the kittens. She should be given light food and plenty of milk.

The kittens are blind when they are born, but should open their eyes when they are ten days old. At five weeks old they should be able to leave their mother.

MAKING AN AQUARIUM

ONE of the first things to know about keeping goldfish and other fish is that they should never, *never* be kept in a plain glass bowl. Fish prefer to live in semi-darkness, and too much light will give rise to all kinds of complaints, notably the dreaded fungus disease which cuts off many a young fish in its prime.

Therefore, if you are thinking of keeping some fish, first make a suitable home ready for them. Instructions are given here for making a tank. This should be placed against a wall, the light, which must not be strong, coming from above, and not entirely from one side, as would be the case if it were placed directly under a window.

As a general rule, the length of an aquarium should be greater than its depth. The tank described here is of average size, having the back and sides opaque and the front transparent.

HOW TO START

Make a base, A, B, C, D, of thick, seasoned wood, measuring thirty inches by fifteen inches, and in this cut four grooves as shown in Fig. 1. The grooves, EG, EF, and FH, should be quarter-inch deep and half-inch wide. EF will be twenty-four inches in length and EG and FH must each measure twelve inches. The remaining groove, GH, will, of course, be twenty-four inches long but, while quarter-inch deep, it must be only eighth-inch wide.

The sides and back of the aquarium must now be cut from half-inch wood. Cut pieces twelve inches wide and of sufficient length to fit flush against the outer edges of the grooves EF, EG, and FH in such a way that the spare eighth-inch of the groove is left inside. The back and sides must be securely screwed and glued at E and F.

Four pieces of glass must now be cut, twelve inches

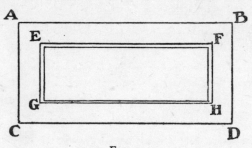

FIG. 1.
Base of the aquarium.

wide and of proper lengths to allow three of them to fit into the remaining portions of the grooves within the sides and back of the aquarium. The fourth piece of glass, exactly twenty-four inches in length, will fit into the narrow groove GH. The fabric of the aquarium will now be entirely glass-lined and appear as in Fig. 2.

Now to make the tank watertight. Make a mixture consisting of three parts pitch and one part gutta-percha, melt it well, and smear liberally over all the joints and places where the water may possibly escape. The floor of the aquarium can also be coated with this mixture. When everything has hardened, fill the aquarium with ordinary tap water and allow to stand twenty-four hours in some dry place. If at

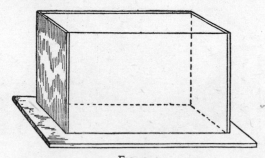

FIG. 2.
The tank with glass lining.

the end of that period there has been no leakage, the tank may be considered perfect, and can be emptied and prepared for its inmates.

THE NEXT STEP

Make some artificial rocks and crevices by placing suitably shaped clinkers against the back and corners of the tank. The floor of the tank can then be covered with fine gravel or clean, washed river sand.

Do not use tap water for the aquarium. Water must be obtained from a stream or pond, as it contains thousands of minute water-plants and water-creatures, which could never be found in tap-water, and these are very important to your fish.

In a general way the water of an aquarium should never be changed, but if, for any particular reason, it should be necessary to empty the tank, this can be done by means of a simple syphon as shown in Fig. 3.

The bent pipe must be filled with water and the ends stopped with corks or the tips of the fingers. One end should then be inserted in the tank and the other

FIG. 3.
Emptying the tank with a syphon.

placed over a receptacle. When the corks or finger tips are removed, the syphon thus formed will empty the tank into the lower vessel.

STOCKING THE TANK

FIG. 4.
Water Crowfoot.

One or two watersnails should live in the tank, as they will keep the water clean ; the fish, too, will eat the snails' eggs.

The plants with which the tank is stocked should be inserted ten days or more before the fish are introduced. One or two plants may be selected from the following, all of which are suitable for a small tank : Water Starwort, Water Crowfoot (Fig. 4), Frogbit, Soldier plant.

150

Water Crowfoot is exceptionally good for a small aquarium on account of its large leaves, which afford shelter and shade for the fish.

FISH TO CHOOSE

Apart from goldfish, carp, tench, minnows, sticklebacks, and golden carp may be kept in a tank. It is wise, however, to choose fish of about the same age and size, otherwise the larger and stronger ones may attack those that are weaker.

It is also advisable not to put " armed " fish like sticklebacks with " unarmed " fish of about the same size or smaller than themselves.

As to food, in addition to the natural food obtained from the water, small worms and ants' eggs are good, and can be purchased from most seed-merchants and pet shops.

FUNGUS

If you should ever notice a white film on one of your fish, remove it at once from the tank (by means of a net), for this is a symptom of fungus disease, which is extremely infectious. Keep the fish in a small tank by itself and give it occasional baths in salted water.

RABBIT KEEPING

RABBITS have become very popular pets—and profitable pets, too, if you keep angoras or chinchillas, for their fur can supply you with quite an amount of extra pocket-money.

This chapter, however, will deal only with the more

Blue Dutch rabbit.

commonly kept rabbits, such as the Blue Dutch (shown here).

When preparing a home for your pets, remember that rabbits in the wild state are used to the warmth of burrows, and therefore the hutches should be placed in a shed where they are sheltered from cold draughts and, what is worse, damp.

Fig. 1 shows a good design for a hutch. For one rabbit of medium size it should measure three feet long and eighteen inches deep and high. The front has a solid door at one end and a wired door at the other,

FIG. 1.
Design for a hutch.

the intermediate portion being a fixed wired frame. The wire netting should be *inside*. If one end is made

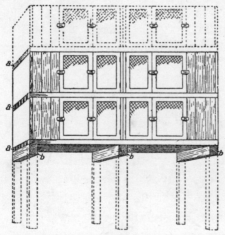

FIG. 2.
Stacked hutches. If you add legs, shown by dotted lines, you might omit the top layer of hutches.

removable as at A, two hutches can be thrown into one. Bore drainage holes at the back corners.

If you need several hutches and make them all to the same pattern they can be stacked in tiers (Fig. 2), separated by wooden battens, one at the front and one six inches from the back, to give room for a gutter under the drainage holes. These gutters are easily made by dividing the " corrugations " of galvanized iron roofing.

The inside of the hutches must be kept clean and fresh with whitewash. While cleaning and white-washing is taking place the rabbits should be removed to another hutch and only returned to their own home when it is absolutely dry. Every year, before winter, the hutches should be thoroughly overhauled and repaired where necessary. Make a practice of sweeping the hutch every day.

Dried grass, hay, bracken, and similar litter are excellent for bedding and should be renewed when necessary.

FOOD FOR RABBITS

Every morning give each rabbit a handful of oats, whole or ground, and a good supply of greenstuff—grass, chicory, sow thistle, dandelion, carrot-tops, lettuce, parsley, leaves of the elm, oak and ash, and twigs with the bark on are examples. Cabbage and broccoli should be given sparingly.

In the evening give bread and milk or meal mash, hay, and any roots obtainable. Rabbits eat most during the night.

In cold weather you may give them a warm mash of potatoes, peas, and meal, but care must be taken to see that the mixture is only warm—not hot.

Rabbits do not need much water, but you may give each about two tablespoonfuls once a week.

EXERCISE

Whenever you can, in dry weather, let your rabbits exercise in a run in the garden. You can easily make one of wire netting on a framework of wood, and the exercise will be good for them.

It is very important that you should place in the hutch something that the rabbits can gnaw and scratch, otherwise they will exercise their teeth and claws on the hutch and possibly make holes in it. Give them a small branch of a tree and they will never suffer from long claws or teeth that have grown so much that it is impossible for them to eat.

HANDLING

If you asked some people how a rabbit should be picked up they would reply, "Oh, by its ears of course!" but to lift a rabbit by its ears alone is very cruel.

To pick up one of your pets, grasp it as shown in Fig. 3, your right hand holding it by the scruff of the neck or the ears and your left hand taking most of the

FIG. 3. *How to lift a rabbit.*

animal's weight at the bottom of its back.

BIRDS

AN aviary is a tremendously interesting thing to possess. If you are anxious to keep birds such as budgerigars (or love birds), canaries, and Java sparrows,

FIG. 1.
An easily made aviary.

you can easily make an aviary in your garden, particularly if you happen to have a sunny greenhouse.

Artificial heat is necessary for several kinds of foreign birds, but so many varieties can stand our English winter in the climate of a conservatory that, as a general rule, the question of stoves may be ignored.

Very little need be done to convert one end of a greenhouse into a large cage, as shown in Fig. 1. Wire netting of a fairly close texture must be stretched from the roof to the ground, leaving an interior space of about thirty-six inches in depth.

A door should be made in the network, as this enables the cage to be entered and thoroughly cleaned, while at the same time it provides the means to enter and catch the birds when necessary.

The floor of the aviary should be covered with very fine gravel and one corner should be turfed. If you have space to do so, plant a small tree, so that the birds may play among its branches. In any case, you should provide odd branches and twigs for them.

If possible cover the walls and back of the cage with virgin cork, the many holes and crevices of which supply excellent sites for nests.

PERCHES

Whether you keep your birds in cages or an aviary, you must exercise particular care in the choice of perches. They must be oval in shape, never round. A glance at Fig. 2 will explain the reason. If the perch is round, the strain upon the muscles of the bird's legs is

FIG. 2.
Make the perches oval, not round.

so great that in many cases a kind of paralysis is caused, whereas oval perches enable the bird to stand with the muscles in a natural and easy state of tension.

As regards the number of birds to an aviary, a good rule is to allow two birds to every foot of frontage ; for instance, an aviary three feet in length should contain not more than six birds.

FEEDING

The majority of birds may be fed upon a diet made up of equal portions of hemp, charlock, millet, and canary seed. A second dish composed of bread-crumbs, wholemeal, and a little finely chopped fat may be given as a treat on special occasions. Apples, watercress, and a few nut kernels can also be used as a second course and will be greatly appreciated by the birds.

The old-fashioned plan of putting a rusty nail in the water-pan is a good way of administering the necessary quantity of iron.

In winter, when the birds are apt to feel the cold, it is most essential that they should be kept well supplied with food. As soon as evening sets in, place a lantern near the seed-pans so that the light falls upon the food and enables the birds to come and eat as often as they wish during the night. An ordinary " bull's eye " will serve this purpose well.

In war-time it is often difficult to obtain the usual bird seed mixtures, and it is illegal to feed birds on oats, rye, or barley, so it is a good idea to grow suitable seeds in your own garden, and to gather and store seeds of dandelions and plantains or "rats' tails." Canaries and budgies are fond of these, and also of groundsel and chickweed plants.

The R.S.P.C.A. has issued a sheet of suggestions that will be helpful, and a copy can be obtained from any branch of the Society.

THE BIRDS' BATHROOM

Freshly filled baths must be placed in the aviary every day, as birds are very clean in their habits, and soon feel the need of a daily dip. Ordinary earthenware pans, holding at least two inches of water, will make excellent baths, and should be placed on the floor where a little splashing can do no harm.

WILD BIRDS

If you live on the outskirts of a town or in the

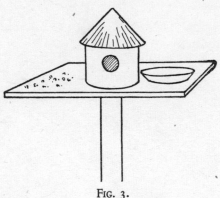

FIG. 3.
One type of bird table.

country you can encourage many different kinds of wild birds to come to your garden if you make a

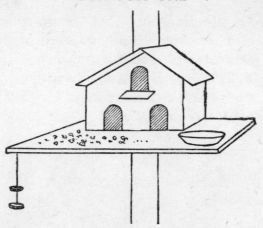

FIG. 4.

This table could be built on to any existing pole or post,
out of reach of cats.

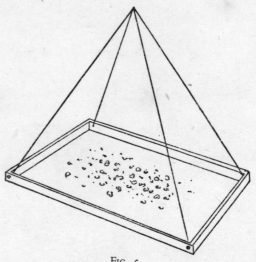

FIG. 5.
Bird tray made from a box lid.

practice of putting food out for them regularly,
summer and winter ; especially in the winter.

It is not always enough to scatter food on the ground, for if there are cats about, no bird will come near. A bird table or tray, placed in a spot where cats cannot reach it, is a better idea.

Two types of bird tables are shown here in Figs. 3 and 4 ; the birds can eat on the platforms in complete safety. In order to attract as many varieties of birds as possible, provide a varied menu—crumbs, bacon rinds, and any kind of fat, coconut and grain of all kinds. Large sunflower heads too, if hung up, will probably bring a number of the finch family to gobble the seeds, and should you have holly berries or rose hips for Christmas decorations, collect the berries later and put them on your bird table for the thrushes and blackbirds. Do not for-

get a vessel of fresh water for drinking and bathing.

If making a bird table is rather outside the range of your carpentery, fix up a tray instead, as shown in Fig. 5. This is best hung from a tree or from projecting pieces of wood fixed to a window frame.

Half an empty coconut shell makes a good container for blue-tit's food. The actual flesh of the coconut is not good for tits, being indigestible, so scoop it out and fill the shell with any scraps of fat, melted and poured in while warm. Bore a hole in the shell and hang it up by a string, choosing a tree within sight of a window if possible, as the antics of the birds enjoying their feast are most amusing.

NEST BOXES

If you would like the birds to nest in your garden and bring up their young ones there, make some nest boxes which you can fix to the trunks of trees. Some suggestions are given in Fig. 6, and the diagrams show clearly how the boxes are made. Note the detachable lids, which enable you to clean the boxes in the autumn, ready for the occupants who will arrive in the spring.

The holes for the birds to go in should always slope upwards into the box, so that no rain can enter. The tits' box should have a hole much smaller than the others, otherwise it will be commandeered by a sparrow or some

FIG. 6.

Some nest boxes. Two have removable lids; the side of the third can be lifted off.

other larger bird. A tit can get through a hole little larger than a half-crown. Make a small perch just below the hole on the outside of the box.

The nest box should blend with its surroundings. Thus, if it is to be fixed to the side of a tree, it should be covered with bark.

Be sure to fix the nest boxes on the sheltered side of the tree.

REARING SILKWORMS

THIS is an interesting hobby that will give you very little trouble.

The best time to start is in April or May, when the eggs can be bought very cheaply at pet shops and in the naturalist department of big stores.

There is no need to make hutches and kennels for silkworms ! Place the eggs in paper trays or boxes—collar-boxes are good for the purpose—and keep them in a fairly cool place, where they are perfectly dry and the eggs can hatch in peace ; make some holes in the top of the box.

THE FOOD SUPPLY

A supply of leaves must be obtained so that the worms may begin to feed directly they hatch. Mulberry leaves are undoubtedly the best, but if you cannot get these, feed your worms on dandelion or blackcurrant leaves. You must keep to the same food throughout ; do not give them dandelion leaves one day and blackcurrant leaves the next.

Some silkworm keepers give their worms lettuce leaves, but these are so succulent that the worms are apt to eat too many and often die of the effects.

A fresh supply of leaves must always be at hand. They should be carefully dried, and no remains from one meal allowed to stand over until the next, as it is most important that the diet should be perfectly fresh.

GROWING UP

A week after hatching, silkworms undergo their first moult, and prepare for this by a day's fasting. The old skin is sloughed in the same fashion as that of a snake, every portion, down to the very jaws, being cast aside.

The new skin being soft, the silkworms grow rapidly until, at the end of another week, the second moult takes place. It is not until these changes have occurred four times that the silkworms attain their full size. At each

FIG. I.
Silkworm at maturity.

change of skin they grow considerably, until at maturity they measure about three inches in length, are almost white, and appear as illustrated in Fig. I.

SPINNING THE COCOON

Ten days or so after its final moult, the silkworm will begin to grow uneasy and will wander about the tray or box seeking a corner in which to spin its cocoon. It is always possible to tell when this stage has been reached, from the transparent appearance of the worm, this being caused by the silky substance or fluid collected in its body. On exposure to the air this fluid hardens into tiny threads as the caterpillar emits them from its mouth.

It will now be time to move the silkworms from their trays and place them in small conical paper bags, as shown in Fig. 2, which can be easily made from notepaper.

It is best to avoid moving the worms with the fingers. When small they can be picked up with a fine camel's-hair brush and, when large, they should be coaxed on to a piece of paper upon which they can be moved.

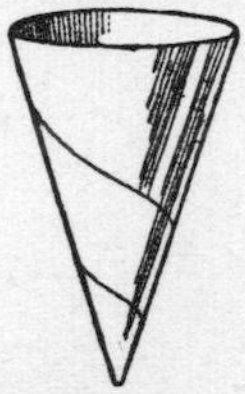

FIG. 2.
Cocoon bag.

When once the worms have been placed each in a paper cone, they set to work spinning their silken cocoons, and after ten days the silk will be quite ready for unwinding. Before unfastening the cone, however, it should be shaken ; if the caterpillar, which has now become a chrysalis, is heard to rattle within, it may be taken as a sign that the cone can be undone.

FIG. 3.
The Cocoon.

The cocoon, when extracted from the paper cone, is about the size of a pigeon's egg and appears as in Fig. 3. This ball is composed of one continuous thread of silk, perhaps 1,000 feet in length, which is wound round and round.

WINDING THE SILK

The cocoon must be placed in a hot oven or in boiling water, in order to kill the chrysalis inside, since if this were left alive it would eat its way out through the silk and entirely spoil it. The hot water also serves to soften the gummy outer covering and loosen the strands of silk within.

Take off the loose outer silk before beginning to

unwind the strands. Several cocoons should be wound at the same time, so that when the ends of the strands have been found they may be placed together and wound on a reel.

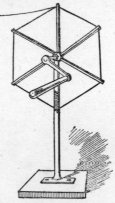

Wooden winders, similar to that shown in Fig. 4, can be bought or made, and will serve to wind the silk as it is unwrapped from the cocoon.

Of course, the silk is raw, and must undergo several processes before it can be woven or adapted to any use, but the beautiful glossy

FIG. 4.
A Silk-winder.

threads, pressed between the leaves of a book, will last for years.

Part III

OUT OF DOORS

PLAYING RED INDIANS

HOWEVER small your garden may be, try to find space in it for a wigwam or a tepee . . . there is nothing as jolly for summer-time, and it will be fun to make your own.

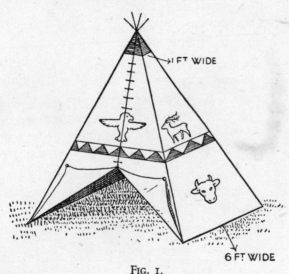

Fig. 1.

How to make a square tepee.

Unbleached calico or old sheets make good covering, and for a square tepee, four poles, lashed together near the top, will be necessary. For a cone-shaped wigwam thirteen poles are needed.

If plenty of material is available each of the sides

should be six feet wide at the base and one foot wide at the top, and six feet high, but naturally you will have to make do with whatever you can get, and a great deal of fun can be had with a tent very much smaller than this. Before erecting it the cover must be decorated with Indian emblems in vivid colours. It is best to sketch the design first, either in full size on paper, or with charcoal actually on the material. You will find that bold designs look better than small niggly ones.

THE DECORATIONS

Enamel or artists' oil colours, the latter thinned with a little turpentine, are the best to use. When applying, first outline the design very lightly to prevent the paint running. If your tent is made from dark material it is a good plan to give the design an undercoat of white, which can either be proper undercoating, which is very cheap, or ordinary white paint or enamel. Allow this first coat to dry thoroughly before applying the second, and do not attempt to make the wigwam or tepee until the paint is quite dry, or you will spoil the whole thing.

DRESSING THE PART

Having made the tepee, you will need a Redskin costume ; this you can make from hessian, which is very inexpensive and is a good substitute for the leather worn by real braves and squaws. Fray out the hems, side seams, and sleeve seams to form the fringe which is characteristic of Red Indian clothing. Very important to a brave is his head-dress of eagle feathers, each feather of which has been awarded to him for some great deed—hence the expression " a feather in his cap." The headband should be made of soft

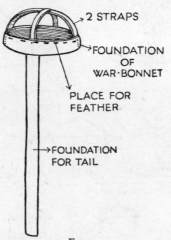

FIG. 2.
Foundation for feather head-dress.

leather, as shown in Fig 2. To this foundation are attached some twenty quill feathers, each with the tip dyed black. Similar feathers are fastened to the " tail."

PICTURE MESSAGES

As many Indian tribes use picture writing, you might like to keep a diary in this novel way, drawing a record of all the important things that happen in or around your tepee. The Indians use all sorts of signs, such as those you see on the following pages, and you can make up your own.

The picture writing shown in Fig. 3 are messages drawn by a boy named Dick, who used the little bird

to represent himself, and will show you the kind of
thing to aim at.

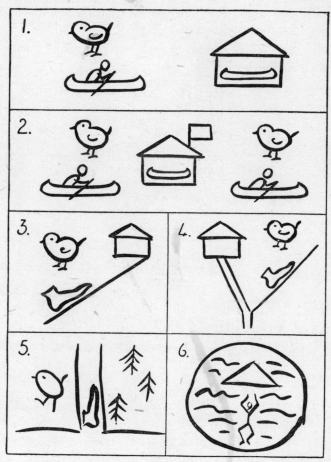

FIG. 3.
Some picture messages.

In No. 1, Dick has paddled to a boat-house. In
No. 2, Dick, still paddling his canoe, passed another
boat-house, where a flag is flying. In No. 3, Dick is

no longer in his canoe, but is on foot and is going uphill towards a hut. In No. 4, Dick is still going uphill, but instead of going direct to the hut he is taking a little path which branches off to the right. In No. 5, Dick is going up a path which is at right-angles to the previous one. There are trees to the right side of the road. In No. 6, the circle represents a pond. There is an island on the pond, and somebody, not Dick, because his sign is not there, is swimming to the island.

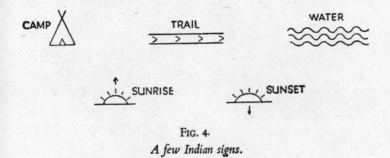

FIG. 4.
A few Indian signs.

AROUND THE COUNTRYSIDE

ONE of the most enjoyable ways of spending any fine day at any time of the year is to go for a walk in the country.

If " going for a walk " sounds horribly dull to  you and means walking aimlessly along a road or a lane with nothing in particular to see, that is a sure sign that you do not set about it in the right way. There is always plenty to see, whether the season is spring, summer, autumn, or winter ; whether the day be sunny or with angry clouds running before the wind. Put on your stoutest, most comfortable shoes and take a bus ride to the edge of the town—or even to the park—and you will soon find plenty to interest you.

TREES AND FLOWERS

First of all, can you name each tree as you come to it ? Do you know the difference between an elm and an oak, except that one has acorns on it in the autumn ? Can you tell from the leaves whether that chestnut tree grows sweet chestnuts that you can

176

eat—or "conkers"? The pictures of trees and leaves in this chapter will help you to recognize those which you are most likely to meet during your walk.

Look out, too, for wild flowers in the fields and

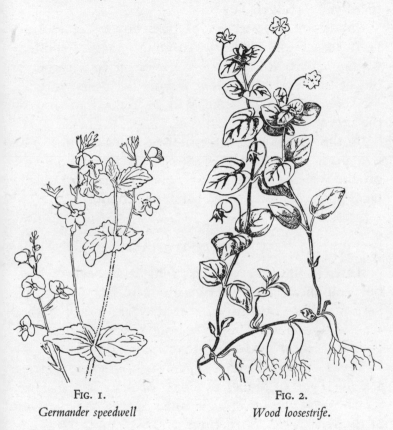

FIG. 1.
Germander speedwell

FIG. 2.
Wood loosestrife.

hedges. Do not pick large bunches of them, though, for if every one did so the lanes would soon be robbed of much of their beauty. Instead pick just one specimen of each kind to take home and press between blotting-paper and mount in an album.

177

The lovely blue speedwell grows on hedge banks and in woods during May and June, but you should only pick this if you are close to your home, for it fades very quickly. Some country folk call the speedwell " Angels' eyes."

While on the subject of blue flowers, a glorious sight to see on an early summer walk is sunshine slanting down through new leaves on to a carpet of bluebells. You will know if you are near bluebells, for their wonderful scent will be carried to you on the breeze.

In the woods watch for the wood loosestrife. This is a plant with yellow flowers. It creeps along the ground, sending out roots as it goes, so that it gradually takes possession of a large patch of ground.

AUTUMN IN THE LANES

Later in the year you will find berries everywhere, but you should take very great care not to eat any berries unless you know what they are and that they are not poisonous. Some poisonous berries look very tempting, so, if in doubt, leave them alone !

Haws, those clusters of small, bright red berries, are the fruit of the hawthorn or may tree. Hips, which grow singly and are much larger, are the fruit of the wild rose. Sometimes you will find, straggling all over a hedge and twining round trees, a vine-like plant whose fruit is attached to soft plumes. The general effect is rather as though someone had strewn cottonwool over the hedge. This plant is called Traveller's Joy or Old Man's Beard. You will find it difficult to gather a specimen, however, unless you have a knife with you, as the feathery parts soon shatter.

Elderberries, in deep purple clusters, are good for

FIG. 3.
Blackberries.

jam. So, of course, are blackberries, and little mistake can be made about these ! Look, too, for sloes, the fruit of the blackthorn. They are somewhat like tiny plums, almost black, with a velvety bloom. It is not wise to eat them, as they are very bitter and will probably give you a pain.

BIRDS

Watch for the birds on your rambles. You will no doubt be able to recognize some of the commoner ones, such as the chirpy little robin with his reddish-orange breast. He loves to perch on a gate-post, the spike of a fence, or anything similar. The thrush also is well known ; he is fairly large and light-brown, and his breast is spotted. You may be lucky enough to see a wagtail—a bird who tells you his name by

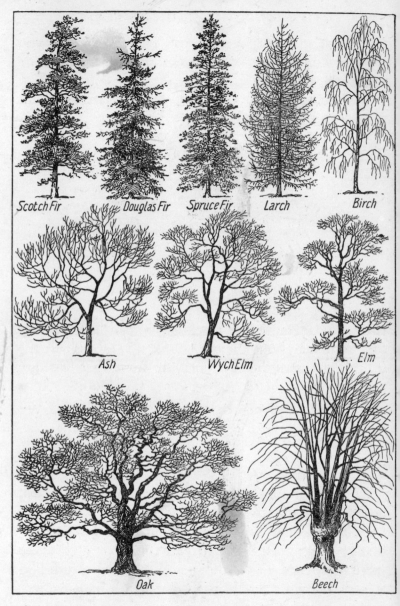

Scotch Fir   Douglas Fir   Spruce Fir   Larch   Birch

Ash   Wych Elm   Elm

Oak   Beech

FIG. 4.

Characteristic winter forms of some of the commoner British trees.

180

Alder Elm Lombardy Poplar Lime Beech Oak Ash Sycamore Maple Hornbeam Plane Horse Chestnut Birch Sweet Chestnut

FIG. 5.

The leaves of common varieties of British deciduous trees.

181

wagging his tail all the time ! In summer he is black-and-white all over, with white cheeks and forehead, and black chin and throat ; but in winter he changes and becomes grey instead of black on the back, and his chin and throat become white.

Many more birds could be described here if there were sufficient space, but any one who is really interested in them should buy a small book on the subject and carry it around when out for a walk, so that each newly discovered bird can be identified. *Birds* in Nelson's "Shown" Series is very useful for this purpose, and gives forty-eight coloured plates.

WHOLE DAY RAMBLES

Well, now that you have had your introduction to the countryside you are sure to want to venture farther afield, and a whole day's walk can be a real adventure. The most adventurous part of it is to choose your route from a map, and if you do not want to lose yourself, you should make a point of studying a suitable map and learning how to read it.

The ideal map for walking has a scale of one mile to the inch. This will be big enough to show the footpaths as dotted lines, so that you need not keep to the road all the time. Most maps have a guide at the bottom, which explains the various signs used on the map, but the illustration given in Fig. 6 will also help you.

One of the first things to learn is how to read the contour lines, which show how many feet you are above sea-level. When these are shown close together it means that a steep hill lies ahead. Study also the different signs for a church with a tower and a church with a steeple, for churches can often be seen for many miles and are first-rate landmarks.

WHAT TO WEAR

Having made yourself familiar with the map, see that you are suitably dressed for a long walk—although you should never try to walk more than, say, six or seven miles at first.

Your feet are most important, since they are to carry you. Your shoes should have good stout soles, and they must be very comfortable ; not too loose, though, or you may find yourself with a blister before you have travelled far. Woollen socks are best.

Your clothing should be light, warm (if it is winter), and fairly loose-fitting. Wear a shady hat if the sun is strong, but otherwise, if you are a girl, you will find that a scarf tied over your head is very comfortable.

Take your map, a mackintosh, some sandwiches, fruit, and perhaps a bottle of milk, packed in a rucksack that you can carry on your back, leaving your hands free. You will not need a walking-stick unless you are going to do some blackberrying as well.

It is a good idea to have a small first-aid outfit in your rucksack, so that you can deal with a thorn scratch, an insect bite, or, if need be, a blister. The outfit should include iodine, a length of bandage, some boracic powder (for blisters), and a box of adhesive dressings that you can buy at any chemist's. Put a plaster on any blister as soon as it is felt.

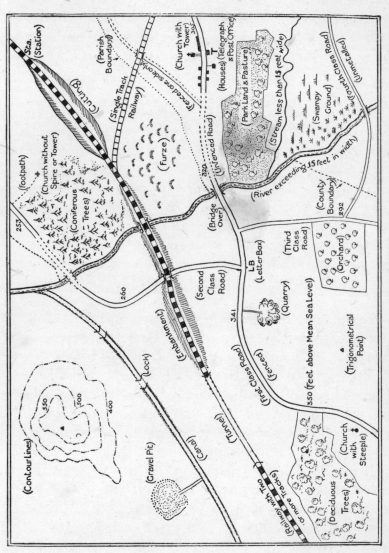

FIG. 6.

184

A WATCH COMPASS

It is easy to find your direction by looking at the sun ; at mid-day it is in the south. Another way is to look at the trees, for moss grows on the south side of the trunk. If, however, you prefer to consult a compass and do not possess one, you can use your watch to find where the north lies.

Hold the watch face upwards, with the *hour* hand (the minute hand does not enter into the calculations) pointing towards the sun.

A line bisecting the angle contained by the hour hand and an imaginary line connecting the centre of the watch with the hour mark at 12, runs due north and south.

Fig. 7.

Using a watch as a compass.

In the diagram the hour hand, at about a quarter past three is pointing to the sun.

LEAF SKELETONS

While you are out, collect a few leaves to take home and make into leaf skeletons for your specimen book. The best way is to use the lime method. Lime can be bought from most colour-merchants and oil shops. Put an ounce or two in an empty jam jar and half fill it with water. Now stand the jar and its contents in a saucepan of water and heat it until the water begins to boil. When the water in the jar also begins to boil, stir it gently but thoroughly with a piece of stick, keeping your face away from the pot to avoid splashes. Then drop in one or two leaves, continuing to stir very gently and taking great care not to touch the leaves.

At the end of two or three minutes take out one of the leaves and place it flat on a level surface (not on any polished wood). With a small mop, made by binding a thickness of rag on to the end of a short cane or knitting-needle, gently rub the surface of the leaf. It will be found that the green part comes away, leaving the delicate tracery of veins beneath.

Having cleaned the green part from one side, turn the leaf over and repeat the process on the other, until nothing but the white skeleton remains.

If the fleshy green substance is difficult to remove, put the leaf back into the jam jar and boil for a trifle longer. Do not leave it there too long, or the lime will attack and destroy the veins.

WASH THE SKELETONS

Wash the skeletons thoroughly in cold water and press them between sheets of white blotting-paper until quite dry and flat, when they are ready to be mounted.

The best way to display and store the skeletons is to mount them on black paper, each fixed into position by a small band of black passe-partout paper. Albums used for photographs and having black paper leaves can often be bought quite cheaply. A sheet of cellophane paper to guard each page is also to be recommended if the book is to be handled a great deal. Print the name of the tree below the specimen, using white paint.

The best leaves to skeletonize are holly, laurel, willow, walnut, rose, beech, and ivy leaves, which make the most beautiful skeletons. Pick the leaves on a dry day in August or September and choose only perfect specimens.

You will soon have a fine collection to remind you of happy days in the open air.

TWIGGY WHISTLE

It is easy to make a whistle from a little twig that you could cut from almost any tree. It is best to choose a small piece of branch that is green, for then the bark comes away easily. The twig might be about five inches long.

As a first step, cut it straight across one end, and then cut a slanting piece away, as in Fig. 8. This will provide the lip of the whistle. Now make a notch at the top side of the lip, as in Fig. 9. Cut a ring right round the bark at the other end of the twig about three inches or so away from the lip.

You must now get away the bark from the lip end of the twig like this : Dip the twig into a little water, and then, using the handle of your penknife as a hammer, start to beat the bark. Do this very carefully so as not to injure the piece of bark, and presently you will be able to pull it off all in one hollow tube. You must now enlarge the notch you made in the twig so that it resembles that in Fig. 10. Next take away a very thin strip of the wood on the top between the notch and the lip. It now only remains to replace

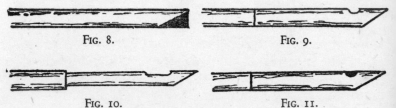

FIG. 8.   FIG. 9.

FIG. 10.   FIG. 11.

Making a whistle from a twig.

the tube of bark that you took off, and the whistle appears as in Fig. 11.

The whistle, when it is blown, should give a fine clear note. If the results are not quite satisfactory, it may be that the notch is not large enough, or perhaps the slip of wood that has been cut away is not sufficiently deeply cut.

WITH MORE NOTES

It is not difficult to make a whistle pipe that will give several notes. In this case a longer twig will be needed, one about nine inches answering the purpose. When loosening the bark several round holes must be cut at intervals down the stick. Then, when the bark is taken away, the notches must be extended farther down the stick. Take thin strips from the wood in between the notches after removing the bark. The whistle is played by closing all the holes with the fingers except the one from which a note is required.

CYCLING

OF course, any enthusiastic rambler scoffs at cycling—just as most cyclists think that they have chosen by far the better hobby. However, it is quite possible to combine both cycling and walking by cycling to a point some miles away, leaving your bicycle at a convenient garage and then going on by foot.

If you are going to have a bicycle, buy the highest-grade machine you can afford. The harder and rougher the use, the better should the bicycle be.

CHOOSING A MOUNT

You may hear of someone who has a second-hand machine to sell, but this, in spite of a no doubt presentable appearance, should be eyed warily. Do not decide to buy it until you have inspected it thoroughly and given it a good trial. If you do not know much about bicycles, any cyclist friend would be flattered if he were asked to help you.

Most modern cycles can be ridden comfortably and yet enable the rider to put at least one foot to the ground without leaving the saddle when he halts. Roughly speaking, the frame, which is the distance from the centre of the bottom bracket to the top of the tube into which the saddle-pillar fits, should be ten inches less than the length of the rider's leg from fork to sole—it may be less, but not more.

A comfortable saddle is very important. It must be wide enough and sufficiently resilient. There are several types of good saddle available. Practically all the leather-topped saddles have an adjusting nut under the peak, to tighten up the tension of the leather when it begins to sag. It is advisable to make use of this nut as soon as any slackness develops, instead of waiting

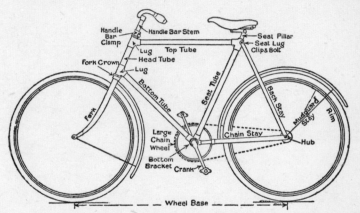

This sketch shows how the different parts of a bicycle are named.

until the leather has sagged on to the springs. Spring-seat saddles have a mattress-like chassis covered with rubber, leather, or leather-cloth, and are specially comfortable.

Whether of the upturned pattern or of the dropped, the handlebars should be at least as wide as the measurement across the rider's shoulders. The position of the grips should be such that the rider's weight is shared between saddle and handlebars, but his arms and back should be straight, forming an inverted V.

The choice of gears is important. When the pedals of a cycle have been turned through one revolution the rear cycle wheel will have revolved more than once ; in other words, the cycle is geared up. The extent of this gearing is expressed in a rather curious way. Suppose the cycle wheel is twenty-six inches in diameter, and that one revolution of the pedal crank causes the cycle wheel to revolve three times. The normal way of expressing this would be to say that the gear ratio is one to three (1 : 3), but the cyclist would say that the machine has a gear of seventy-eight, because one turn of the pedals will make it travel the same distance as it would with one revolution of the wheels if they were seventy-eight inches in diameter.

The higher the gear, the greater the distance the cycle travels for each turn of the pedals, but the effort required to turn the pedals is greater. A normal gear of sixty is very suitable for general use, and if that be used in conjunction with a standard Sturmey-Archer three-speed hub it will give a top gear of eighty and a forty-five bottom, which will provide for easy and difficult conditions of riding. It is a mistake to ride in the highest gear possible. A better principle is to use the lowest that can be pedalled comfortably, and to change up when the rate of pedalling becomes too fast.

Reliable brakes are essential, as your life may at some time depend on their efficiency. Two good brakes should be carried, and they must be kept in perfect working order.

Mudguards should be fitted. Steel and celluloid are the usual materials of which they are made. Steel is the stronger, but is inclined to rattle unless the guards are kept perfectly rigid at all points of attachment ; it also has the disadvantage of rusting whenever the enamel is scratched. Celluloid guards are light and cannot rust, but they are easily bent or broken if carelessly treated. As it is the law that at night cyclists must have a red rear light or a red reflector and a white surface, it is as well to fit a white rear mudguard or one made of aluminium or chromium plated.

ON TO THE ROAD

Having bought your bicycle, take it on to a quiet road and learn to ride it. With the modern low-built cycles it is not necessary for the rider to learn to mount and dismount from the saddle. It is much easier and safer to lift the right leg over the saddle or handlebars while the cycle is at rest. For the same reason it is easy for anyone to learn to ride a bicycle without assistance. If the saddle is lowered the rider can reach the ground with both feet, and so will be able to hold the machine up without assistance until he has acquired the trick of balance. Actually, most people learn to balance on two wheels at an early age by riding " fairy cycles." What they sometimes do not learn is the importance of " ankling."

By making full use of the ankle joints the cyclist can cover greater distances with less fatigue than if he merely pushes the pedals down with alternate thrusts of the legs. Skill in the important art of " ankling " at first calls for determined practice, but it well repays the trouble. At the top of the stroke the foot is inclined upwards, so that the pedal can be pushed forward and downward (not merely stamped down). As the foot moves downwards it changes its inclination by movement at the ankle-joint until, when it reaches the bottom of its stroke, the toes are pointing downwards. This enables the pedal to be "pulled" round and partly lifted on the upward stroke. Then the weight of the foot is slightly lifted,

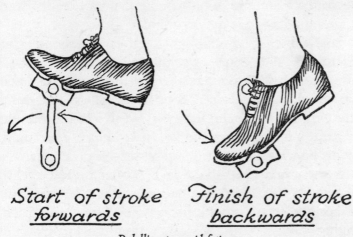

Start of stroke forwards   Finish of stroke backwards

Pedalling to avoid fatigue.

so that the rising pedal does not have to carry the foot with it, and the toes are again pointed upwards. The foot is then ready for the next forward and downward stroke.

After dropping to a lower gear do not quicken the pedal rate unduly. When rounding a sharp corner on a greasy road have the outside pedal full down, so that the leg on the inside of the curve may be free to support you in case of a sideslip. During a long ride a slight alteration of the height of the saddle relieves the leg muscles. Another point to remember is that it is no loss of dignity to get off and push your bicycle up a steep hill ! You will only tire yourself out by pedalling laboriously to the top.

YOUR CYCLING KIT

Like walking, cycling gives you the freedom of the countryside and soon you will undoubtedly want to take longer trips farther afield.

For winter cycling over long distances, the conventional " plus four " cycling suit is ideal for both boys and girls, as it combines ease and comfort with maximum warmth. A divided skirt, or culotte, is another great favourite for girls' wear. In the summer practically all boys, and most girls, like to wear shorts for cycling.

You should also invest in a proper oilskin cycling cape and a sou'wester ; these are quite cheap and can be bought from practically any cyclists' store. The cycling cape should be long enough to come well down over the handlebars, and it should have thumb tapes on it so that you can hold it down as you hold the handlebars. When it is wet, dry it thoroughly by arranging it over the seat and back of a chair, in front of a fire.

SOME GENERAL HINTS

Oil your bicycle fairly often, but apply only a little oil at a time. When you have been riding through muddy roads and come home with mud spattered all over the machine, wipe it off while it is still wet, and polish up the machine next day when it has had time to dry. A rag damped with paraffin oil or French polish smartens up the enamel.

Your rear tyre should be pumped fairly hard—though not board-hard, but the front tyre should be considerably softer.

LUBRICATING

Every moving part of a bicycle should be kept well oiled at the points where it rubs against a stationary part. Not all these points are provided with oilers or oil-gun nipples, but they should not be overlooked. A little oil at frequent intervals is the best principle, and the cycle maker's instructions should be carefully followed, as different parts of a cycle need different kinds of oil.

THE CHAIN

A properly adjusted chain should have no more than one inch of up-and-down play when tested at a point mid-way between the chain-wheel and the rear sprocket. It should not, however, be tight.

A worn chain will be tighter at some places than others. To adjust the tension on the chain, unscrew the nuts which lock the ends of the rear wheel spindle to the frame, and then move the wheel forwards and backwards in the fork slots. On the roadster type of machine there will be two chain adjusters fitted in the fork-ends ; by turning the small nuts on them the wheel spindle may be moved in either direction. Finally, screw the spindle nuts up tightly again.

OFF YOU GO !

Having armed yourself with this knowledge of your bicycle, you can take the road without a care in the world—and miles of countryside, ancient towns, and old-world villages lie before you, waiting to be explored.

When you are going off on a long cycle run you will find the rambler's one-inch-to-the-mile map very useful, but it is well to take the map that adjoins, just in case you ride off one on to the other ! Some cyclists prefer a map which has a scale of four miles to the inch.

While it is quite possible to ride comfortably with your belongings in a rucksack on your back, a better idea is to have a roomy saddle-bag. If you are off on a cycling week-end, perhaps camping or visiting Youth Hostels, panniers would be a good investment. These are twin bags which hang from your carrier on either side of your back wheel ; you can stow a great deal of stuff in them, including sleeping-bag and night necessities.

PHOTOGRAPHY

WHAT wonderful moments you can capture with a camera ! That bough of apple blossom spreading against the sky, that comical, inquiring twist of your dog's head, that lovely bend in the stream where the cattle come to drink, the sails of a fishing-boat silhouetted against the setting sun, and many others.

A camera is a great asset when you are off for a ramble or a cycle ride, for you can bring back snaps that will form the perfect diary of your adventures. This habit of taking photographs of everything that seems to make a "picture" forms, too, an excellent method of gaining experience for a beginner, such varied work laying the foundation of general photographic knowledge and preparing the way for specialized studies.

LOFTY AMBITIONS

After a certain time, however, if the art of the camera interests you in itself, you will probably want—without altogether giving up your snapshot diary—to try as well as this some more advanced work, and to aim at producing such artistic photographs that they have some claim to be considered as pictures. If this is your ambition you would be well advised to make a speciality of one particular line—

perhaps two—instead of indiscriminately attempting all and sundry. You will gradually gain a store of practical knowledge about exposures, distances, backgrounds, focus, etc., that will give you a better chance of success, because more concentrated, than a few preliminary failures in various classes of subjects.

Choose a subject that appeals to you and for which your own neighbourhood offers fairly frequent opportunities. If you live near the coast you will have special advantages for studying magnificent skies, cloud-masses, and the sea in all its aspects ; if you live in the country you will have better opportunity for animal studies and landscapes. Townspeople can find plenty to inspire them in old buildings and quaint corners. Tiny children, not posed, but taken in all kinds of natural attitudes and occupations—playing, eating, crying, laughing, solemn—make charming photographic studies. But take care to " stalk " them almost as carefully as wild birds, for they must be quite unconscious of the camera !

Even indoors and in the garden you will find things to photograph—flowers, trees, leaves, and models against a plain background with the light just so to throw delicate shadows, firelight pictures, and so on.

It is a good plan to keep a photographic notebook and to put in it prints of all your negatives that are worth keeping, entering opposite each print details of the photographic process (exposure, developing, etc.) and notes as to time and weather conditions when the photo was taken. A record of these matters will show you reasons for past failures and successes, and be a great help to you in future attempts.

CHOOSING A CAMERA

Some cameras are made so that when in use they can be held in the hand or fixed on a tripod ; they are made also either with the lens in a fixed position (a fixed-focus camera) or so that it can be adjusted (a focusing camera). For beginners, a reliable make of hand camera of the fixed-focus type is decidedly the best, as it is far less complicated to manage—*e.g.* an ordinary box camera.

FOCUSING

In using any type of camera, you must first see that it is in position to take the picture you want. To make sure of this, you look through the view-finder—the tiny plate of glass in the top of the camera—in which you will see the objects in front of the lens reproduced in miniature.

Move the camera about until the picture you want appears in the view-finder ; with a box camera you can then go ahead and " press the button," for there is practically nothing more to be done. No focusing need be considered because, in a fixed-focus camera, all other objects at any distance beyond your picture are practically as clear as the picture itself.

It is for this reason that a fixed-focus camera is so easy for beginners and so useful for all general kinds of work ; and yet, as you can see, not quite adequate for work which demands much " atmosphere," since it makes nearly everything so clear. Suppose you are photographing a field of flowers. To make an

FIG. 1.

The composition of pictures. Notice how picture (a) is improved, as shown in (b), by taking the snap from a different angle. (d) is an improvement on (c), as the interest is centred in the boats and the picturesque building in the background.

artistic picture, the foreground flowers should stand out individually, those just behind a little less clearly, those in the background blurred into soft cloudy masses. To get such an effect you need a focusing camera with a large lens. With a focusing camera you can alter at will the distance between lens and film (or plate), the whole camera front containing the lens being made to move backwards and forwards on metal runners. With this device, to get the exact focus of the foreground flowers you run your lens backwards or forwards to the desired position. You will find that with this type of camera, when your foreground is sharp there is a softening or blurring at a short distance farther off.

Focusing cameras may have other devices—such as the power to raise or lower the camera front, to alter the lens aperture by minute gradations, etc.—all of which give the photographer greater power, but which are so many stumbling blocks to the mere beginner. When you have served your apprenticeship with the easier type of camera and have gained knowledge and experience of the elementary rules of photography you will then be ready for a focusing camera ; there are many excellent makes ranging in price from about twenty-five shillings to several pounds, according to the quality of the lens and the fittings.

THE CAMERA'S "WORKS"

With any camera, the operations of inserting a roll of films, taking instantaneous snapshots, and removing the roll from the camera when all the films have been exposed, are the least part of the photo-graphic art, being purely mechanical actions that can be learnt easily. Full instructions for this part of the business are enclosed on a printed sheet with each camera sold and should give you no trouble whatever.

EXPOSING THE FILM OR PLATE

When you are not taking snapshots, but are giving a time exposure, you must use your judgment and experience. It is well to realize at the outset that this is one of the great difficulties which will beset you, and to take to heart the following maxim : *correct exposure is the foundation of all good photography*. To expose a film or plate for the right time, you must take into consideration the following things :

1. The intensity of the light.
2. The size of the lens aperture.
3. The speed of the film.
4. The nature of the subject.

The intensity of the light varies with weather, season, and time of day. One gets the greatest intensity of light in brilliant sunshine during the middle hours of the day (from 10 a.m. to 2 p.m.) at the height of summer (June and July). As a rule the more intense the light the shorter the exposure ; if, however, the brilliant light throws strong shadows, this rule must be modified, otherwise you would get shadows without any detail—merely black silhouettes.

The second point for consideration, *the size of the lens aperture,* is also a most necessary factor in getting a correct exposure. In front of the lens there is a " shutter "—that is, an arrangement of thin metal plates, the opening and shutting of which controls the length of exposure given to the film. This shutter is made to work in such a way that it can open and shut at varying speeds, and in conjunction with "stops" which cause the shutter to open partially or completely.

In some first-class focusing cameras the "stops" are very numerous, so that the lens aperture can be reduced by minute alterations of size ; in simple cameras, such as beginners use, there are fewer stops— usually only three. The bigger the lens aperture the shorter the exposure ; the lens to its full extent should, as a rule, be used for instantaneous exposures ; the various "stops" can be used for time exposures, and are specially useful when sharpness of outline is needed.

The stops are referred to in photographic terms by the letter "f" followed by a number—e.g. f.11, f.8, f.22, etc. The shutter has an indicator on which these numbers are marked, and which should be set to the number required ; the higher the number, the smaller the lens aperture.

Speed of the plate or film is another important factor in calculating exposures. Both plates and films are made with varying degrees of sensitiveness—i.e. with varying degrees of speed—and this must be taken into account when deciding on your exposure. Certain cameras will, however, take only one kind of film of standard speed.

The fourth point, *the nature of the subject,* influences the length of the exposure very much. A picture taken on the coast, for example, showing a wide expanse of sea and sky, requires a shorter exposure than one of a country landscape (especially one showing woods or trees), even though conditions of weather,

FIG. 2.

*The upper sketch shows lighting from directly in front. The lower
sketch shows the better effect of side lighting.*

time, and season are identical. In the same way the
country landscape will, unless taken under trees,
require less exposure than one taken in a narrow town

street. The reason for these differences lies in the varying amount of reflected light shown by the three classes of subjects. Again, a snow scene, for the same reason, should not be given a normal winter exposure, the amount of reflected light from snow being very great.

Indoor scenes naturally need a much longer exposure than any of the examples just given, and here again a great variation is required according to circumstance ; a bright sunny drawing-room, for instance, should have a far shorter exposure than the interior of a cathedral. In the latter case the exposure may have to be reckoned by minutes instead of by seconds or fractions of a second, in some very dark churches half an hour being hardly too much.

It is impossible to lay down definite rules for length of exposure, even given certain conditions of light, weather, subject, etc., because the exposure varies with the lens and the stop used. Common sense will tell you, however, that when you are taking moving objects you should use the highest shutter speed possible and open the stop to its fullest extent.

A sound investment is an exposure calculator. There are several types on the market, and one of the best and least expensive is the Wellcome Exposure Calculator, which costs less than two shillings. It is a mine of information and is revised annually.

DEVELOPING

This is the next step after the film or plate has been exposed. It is a process requiring not only great care and some judgment, but a certain amount of apparatus also, and a tank or dark room. Some amateurs shrink from the trouble and uncertainty of the development process, and get their films developed by a professional. This is an easy plan, but it will never make you an amateur photographer really worth the name ! If you have no tank and no space for a dark room, or if your time is limited, you cannot help yourself ; but, where it is at all possible, learn to develop your own negatives, even though you begin by having them developed for you in the first enthusiasm of owning a camera and taking snapshots of everybody. It is not a bad plan to learn the various photographic mysteries gradually.

After exposure, the object photographed, though actually present on the film, is invisible until it has been treated with a proper chemical solution—*i.e.* until it has been developed. This means, of course, that by developing a film you only complete the work already begun by the action of the light ; hence the need, if the developing is to be satisfactory, for a correct exposure first—a fact that is too often forgotten. It should be realized, then, that a correctly exposed film may be ruined by bad development, but that perfect development will not produce a perfect negative if the exposure has been utterly wrong.

The following are the requirements for developing : Developing solution, fixing solution, developing tank or developing dish, a good water supply close at hand.

You may buy the chemicals for the developing solution and make it up yourself, or you may buy the solution ready made and add water as required. As good results depend largely on scientific accuracy of proportion, it is safer for the beginner to buy the ready-made solution, and add water strictly to the quantity directed. Never add the water by guess-work, the result is almost sure to be unsatisfactory.

If you develop by the tank method, there are certain manipulations to be learned in connection with the correct use of each make of tank ; but these are purely mechanical and are fully explained in the printed instructions which accompany the purchase. Tank development can be carried on in daylight, but naturally subdued daylight is to be preferred ; do not attempt it in bright sunshine.

Dish development, whether of plates, flat films, or roll films, needs a dark room. By this is meant a place from which all white light is excluded and which is lit by a ruby-coloured light. Your film, before fixing, would be acted upon by the white light and made foggy ; under red rays it is comparatively safe. Red lamps are supplied by photographic dealers at very moderate prices ; but if the dark room has electric light, round which an adequate red shield can be placed, a photographic lamp will not be needed.

For convenience, a dark room should not have a large window, as it is very difficult to shut off com-pletely a big area of light. A small window can be easily blocked out by a light wooden frame filled in with cardboard and edged all round with felt or baize. There must be no crack or crevice where the light can come in ; be careful to notice if all is well under the door and round the edges of the wooden frame.

When the room is quite ready, put the required amount of developer into the dish and add the necessary amount of water. Then pour out the fixing solution into the fixing dish, which should be a good-sized one, capable of taking the roll of film uncut, or else cut into portions and spread out singly. The fixing liquid is a solution of hypo-sulphate of soda (hypo) and water in the proportion of four ounces of hypo to a pint of water. It is convenient to keep a bottle ready mixed to use as required.

When all these details have been attended to, unwind your film and take it off the spool. Holding an end of the roll in each hand, place the film so that the middle of it rests in the dish well immersed in the developer. Now begin to rock the film gently to and fro by lifting and lowering each hand alternately in a slow continuous movement, so that all parts of the film are successively immersed in the developing fluid. Your great aim must be to secure equal development along the entire length of the exposed part of the film, so the slow continuous movement must be kept up without pause until development is complete ; be careful in each lowering movement of either hand to let all the exposed part of that half of the film get well immersed.

FIG. 3.

Developing a roll film by hand.

When development is complete, and the details are clearly shown, rinse the film in two or three changes of water before fixing.

FIXING

To fix the developed film you may treat it exactly as you have been doing for development—*i.e.* rock it gently and continuously up and down, in and out of the fixing dish. The process must go on until the back of the film is quite clear of the thick creamy coating which covers it ; and after this happens it is safer to continue the rocking for as long again : for example, if it takes ten minutes to clear off the coating, the whole fixing time should be twenty.

If your fixing dish is large enough, or if you have two, you can adopt the less tedious process of plunging the whole film at once in the hypo solution for about ten or twelve minutes, either uncut, if the dish is long enough to take it, or cut up into the exposed portions. Do not, if you cut it into portions, let them lie one over the other, as they are apt to stick together. Do not be afraid either of using plenty of the fixing solution. Hypo is very cheap and it is poor economy to spoil a batch of negatives by being sparing of it.

After fixing, the film must be thoroughly washed to free it from all traces of hypo. This is best done by allowing it to remain in running water ; specially made little tanks fitted with a tap can be bought for this purpose. Failing a tank, wash the film by plunging it into several changes of fresh water in a basin.

When the film is washed it should be hung up to dry ; a length of string stretched taut between two points makes an excellent drying line. The film can be attached to it by a clip, and should be allowed to swing quite free until it is perfectly dry. Do not attempt to hurry the process by putting the film near the fire—there will be dire results if you do ! The gelatine will melt and run, and all your pictures will be distorted out of recognition into grotesque nightmares !

PRINTING

This will give you the actual picture—the result you have been leading up to since the exposure.

For the simplest form of printing you will need a printing frame, any good make of self-toning daylight paper, and, as before, some of the hypo solution used for fixing the negative.

FIG. 4

A useful type of wooden clip for suspending prints while drying. A spring-type clothes peg can be adapted.

Open the frame, place the negative in position, the film side away from the glass. Place a sheet of the paper face to face with the film side of the negative, being careful to see that the sensitive side of the paper is next to the film. Shut up the frame and put it out to print. With the average negative it is best to print in the shade, sunshine printing not giving such a good result except with a very dense negative. The time needed for printing varies enormously with the strength of the light. You can always see how the printing progresses by swinging back one of the catches of the frame and lifting a corner of the printing paper, being careful not to disturb the position of negative or print. The paper must be printed a good deal darker than you want it finally to be, as it loses a good deal of its tone in the fixing bath. Leave it in the hypo solution for about twelve minutes, and then wash it for an hour in running water, or for two hours in several changes of water.

LANDSCAPES

Sometimes very good effects can be got by *almost* facing the camera in the direction of the sun—this softens the outlines and makes a more artistic picture—but care should be taken to shade the lens from the direct rays. Avoid taking exposures in very bright sunlight, as the outlines are so clear that the effect is hard. Don't be afraid of taking landscapes on a misty day, especially if you have some distinct object in the foreground, such as a rock or some animals—most beautiful effects can be obtained in this way ; but realize that a camera magnifies the effect of fog about three times.

PORTRAITS

Do not place your sitters in the sun if you can avoid it—it makes the subject appear to have a scowling expression and gives the features a hard outline. Try not to take people against a very light or white background, it makes the faces appear much darker than they really are, giving quite fair-skinned Saxon types almost an Indian look. A medium, indefinite background is best—grass, distant foliage, old buildings are all good for this purpose.

TRIMMING

Before putting your prints into your album, study them carefully to see whether they might be improved

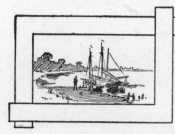

FIG. 5.

Before trimming a print examine it under two adjustable masks like these till the most pleasing effect is obtained.

by trimming—that is, by cutting off perhaps half an inch from the side, top, or bottom, to give the subject greater prominence, or improve the " balance " of the picture.

To judge this, cut two right-angled pieces of card or paper and place them over the snapshot, as shown in the illustration. By sliding them closer together or farther apart you will be able to tell if part of the photograph is unnecessary.

JOINING A CLUB

A very pleasant way of keeping in touch with one's fellow hobbyists is by joining a local photographic club if circumstances make this possible. In addition to the enthusiasm that spreads from one to another, all interested in the same thing, a club has this further advantage, that it sometimes possesses expensive apparatus which can be shared in common by all the members. If you want, for instance, to make experiments in enlarging—a most fascinating by-path of photography, and not at all difficult—the club enlarging outfit would enable you to enjoy this aspect of your hobby without the expense of buying for yourself an apparatus which, in all probability, you might **not** use very often.

SWIMMING

APART from being a very useful pastime, swimming is one which you can indulge in by yourself with almost as much fun as you would have with companions.

The main thing is to be able to swim with confidence so that you need no one at hand to haul you into shallow water. At the same time, you should not bathe in a spot that is too secluded, for if you get into difficulties, there may be no one within earshot to help you out.

If you are one of those " swimmers " who like to keep at least one foot on the bottom, this chapter will help you to master the simpler strokes, while good swimmers may be able to glean a few hints to give them a final polish.

The racing swimming strokes recognized by the universal swimming world come under three classes—the free style (which includes the trudgeon, crawl, and trudgeon-crawl), the breast stroke, and the back stroke.

Practise the strokes while you lie across a table or stool, and you will have more confidence when you enter the water.

THE BREAST STROKE

In learning the breast stroke, the body should lie easily on the surface of the water, the feet a few inches below it, and the lower part of the face immersed a little beneath the water.

Place legs together and straight, toes pointing back, arms fully extended in front of the body, hands touching, fingers closed, and palms downward. In starting to swim the stroke, turn the palms of the hands outwards, thumbs down, and keeping the elbows rigid, bring the arms back just below the surface of the water with a short, vigorous movement, pulling down as well as outwards. The legs are not

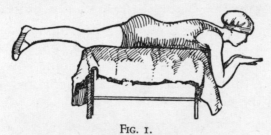

FIG. I.

Breast stroke. Starting position : swimmer inhaling.

moved until the hands approach the breast, then they are drawn up, knees outward and sideways, heels kept as close together as possible, feet pointing backwards and turned outwards.

When the hands begin their forward movement the legs are kicked out straight and away from the body with a vigorous action. On the completion of the full extension of the legs and feet they are brought sharply together with all the speed and power possible, the heels showing above the surface of the water. In this position the body, driven by the impetus of the kick, is allowed to " glide " until the momentum is all but exhausted, when the arms are started again.

Of course, although the various parts of the stroke are described separately, when in action they are connected into one another so closely as to produce a smooth, graceful, progressive action.

Breathing is most important, and should be easy and regular. When traversing a distance of considerable length, a deep full breath at every stroke becomes essential, so far as the conserving of energy is concerned. Breathing is effected immediately before the recovery of the arms, the head and shoulders being lifted out of the water to enable a strong deep breath to be taken.

Breath is exhaled as the swimmer is performing the " gliding " motion, and as in other swimming strokes, is inhaled through the mouth and exhaled through the nostrils.

BACK STROKE

The improvements that have been made in this stroke are of such a radical nature that some swimmers doubt its right to be termed the back stroke. But as the stroke in every respect conforms with the rules and regulations governing it in championship races, swimmers are quite in order in taking up the stroke for speed purposes. In comparing the modern style of back-swimming stroke with the original one, you will find them differing fundamentally in mechanism.

In learning the original plain back stroke, the swimmer had to lie flat on his back on the surface of the water as in floating, with arms at full extension above the head, hands flat, palms turned upwards. This position ended the stroke, and was held so until the swimmer's body had exhausted its " glide " after the leg kick had been made.

In bringing down the arms, the hands, back to back with palms outwards, caught the water sharply and were pulled through it with a long, steady pull, both at the same time, elbows stiff, describing a semi-circle just below the surface and parallel to it. When the arms came alongside the body, palms turned downwards and kept rigid, they were carried to their

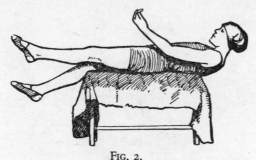

FIG. 2.

Back stroke. First movement: left arm and left leg beginning stroke.

full reach by raising them up well clear of the water. The legs held close together, toes downwards, until the arms began their revolution, then they were drawn up and opened outwards from the body, as in the breast stroke kick, and snapped together as the arms attained their full extension, when the body, now in original position, was let " glide " until the momentum imparted by the kick was exhausted. Then another arm stroke was begun. That was really the action and timing of the original back stroke.

The leg movements of the old and new styles of back stroke are as wide apart, in principle, as the poles.

Whereas the leg kick of the original style was on the lines of the breast-stroke kick, the modern style of the leg kick is the same as used in the free style or plain crawl, that is, that the legs thrash up and down in the water. The arms and legs do not drive and recover together, but with an alternate movement, and the correct position of the head is an important factor in balancing the body for the stroke to be performed correctly. In learning the new style of

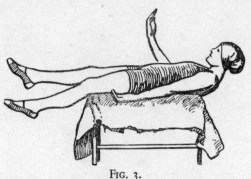

FIG. 3.

Back stroke. Second movement : right arm and right leg being raised for stroke.

back stroke, the position of the body is flat on the back on the surface of the water, as in the old style, the head being raised clear of the water.

The arm action being alternate, each arm starts its movement from alongside the body near the thighs, and is brought upwards fully extended above the head, the palms of the hands being turned outward from the body, and with an easy, relaxed motion ; it is then brought smartly back to the thigh, describing a semicircle a little below the surface of the water.

As one arm finishes its pull the other arm begins.

The timing and co-ordination of the arm and leg movements will prove the most difficult problem for the swimmer to solve. Breathing is the same as in other styles of swimming strokes—inhaling through the mouth and exhaling from the nostrils.

TRUDGEON STROKE

This is the least tiring of swimming strokes, when its relative speed is considered, and may be used for any distance. The best and easiest way to learn the trudgeon leg kick is to make use of the iron rail that

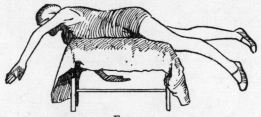

FIG. 4.

Trudgeon stroke. First movement : left arm entering water as legs are opening for kick. Swimmer inhaling.

usually runs round the sides of the swimming bath. Clasp the rail with your right hand, place the palm of the left hand on the side of the bath, underneath the water, immerse your left shoulder under the water, and stretch your body out to its full length. Strike out forwards with the right leg, keeping the leg stiff from the thigh downwards to the tips of the toes. Bring the left leg back to a kneeling position. When the foot of the under leg, the left one, is two or three feet from the heel of the upper one, the legs and feet are brought smartly together.

For the arm movement, let the body rest on the water with the hands at full reach above the head, palms down. The palms of the hands enter the water in a flat position, and the upper arm is brought down and round in a semi-circle with a strong, steady pull, bent a little at the elbow, fingers together, until straight down alongside the body, and the arm is brought forward well above the water. The under arm is started just as the upper arm finishes.

The under arm follows the same semi-circle as the other arm. In swimming this stroke the body rolls strongly, so that breath has to be taken by a rapid turn of the head from the shoulders as the upper arm is entering the water, and exhaled through the nostrils under the water as the body turns face downwards in the water.

THE CRAWL

In the trudgeon stroke, when swum easily, there is a time when the propelling forces pause, the body sinks lower in the water, and a decided check is noticed in the speed of the swimmer, whereas in the crawl stroke the continuous action of the legs keeps the body constantly in motion, so that there is no check or sinking and the stroke must perforce be faster. The smooth combination of the arms and legs and the timing of the stroke are the chief effects to be solved.

First master the leg action thoroughly. Lie flat on the surface of the water, face downwards, arms and body at full stretch, arms motionless above the head, and start to kick the legs up and down alternately, keeping them stiff at the hip and holding the knees close together. There is little difficulty in learning this, because the motion is so simple. When the action of the legs becomes mechanical to you with practice, try to bring your arms and shoulders into action.

When beginning to learn the arm stroke, bring the arms, a little bent at the elbow, to their full length above your head. The arms should be a little more open than in the trudgeon, the hands and fingers

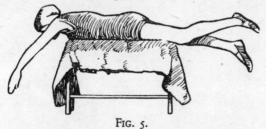

FIG. 5.

Crawl stroke. Left arm entering water as left leg is being raised for downward thrash. Swimmer inhaling.

pointing flat and a shade downwards when about to enter the water.

Bring the arms down and round underneath the water until they reach the thigh, then lift them clear of the water and carry them forward again with the elbow not too high up in the air, in a relaxed position. The action of the arms in completing the motion is in the form of a semicircle. The arms when entering the water should not be more than twelve inches away from the head.

The under arm is started just as the upper one finishes. The position of the body is flat on the face, much as when sprinting with the trudgeon. There should be hardly any rolling, and breath is taken every two or three strokes by a quick twist of the head as the upper arm is being brought down through the water.

TRUDGEON-CRAWL

The trudgeon-crawl swimming stroke is a combination of the trudgeon and crawl strokes, and is divided into two classes, the four-beat and the six-beat.

The four-beat trudgeon-crawl stroke is nothing

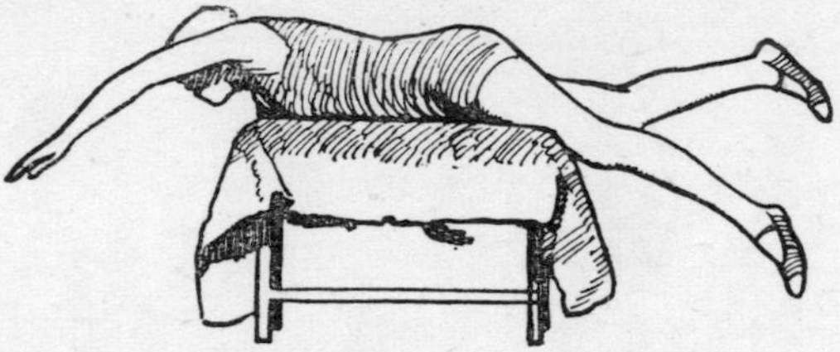

FIG. 6.

Four-beat Trudgeon-crawl. First movement: left arm entering water as legs are opening for narrow trudgeon leg kick. Swimmer inhaling.

more than a trudgeon narrow thrash leg kick on the side upon which, whether left or right, the swimmer inhales his breath, and two plain leg crawl kicks, as the swimmer is bringing his arm over on what is known in swimming circles as his " blind side," combined with the ordinary trudgeon arm stroke.

The leg action is the first to be learned. The easiest way to learn it is as follows : Enter the water and place each hand, palm downwards, on the rail at the side of the bath. Stretch the body to its full length, face downwards, in the water, and start to perform the simple leg kick of the plain crawl stroke, counting one, two, three, four as the legs and feet thrash the water up and down alternately, with a decided emphasis on the *four*.

You count one, two, on the side upon which you turn to inhale your breath, and three and four of the leg beats are performed as the swimmer exhales breath underneath the water, as in the trudgeon stroke.

Then start to take up the timing of the leg beats to the arm stroke. You must bear in mind that there

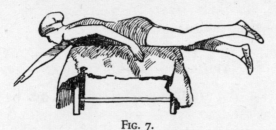

FIG. 7.

Four-beat Trudgeon crawl. Second movement: right arm entering water as legs and feet are performing their plain crawl kick. Swimmer exhaling.

are two distinct leg beats to each arm stroke. Let us suppose that you are a right over-arm swimmer. As you begin to bring your right arm over, at the same time inhaling your breath, you must thrash the water downwards with the right leg first, counting *one*, then thrash the water downwards with the left leg, counting *two*, as the right arm enters the water.

Then, as you turn over face downwards to exhale your breath underneath the water and begin to bring your left arm over, you must thrash the water downwards with your right leg, counting *three*, and then thrash downwards with the left leg, counting *four*, as the left arm enters the water.

Now the rolling of your body from side to side, which is inevitable if you wish to perform the stroke correctly, causes your legs to assume a slightly slanting position on the count of the leg beats one and four, which compel you to describe a trudgeon short, narrow, thrash leg motion. The stroke should be an easy, comfortable, and very smooth stroke. The movements of the legs and feet should be rapid, and the thrash not too violent. The arm stroke is slower than in the plain crawl stroke, and is the same as performed in the trudgeon stroke.

TRUDGEON-CRAWL SIX-BEAT

The six-beat trudgeon-crawl stroke can be learned rather on the lines of the four-beat stroke. The only difference from the four-beat is that there are three distinct leg beats to each arm stroke, or six leg beats to the movement completed by both the swimmer's arms, and the arm action is a little slower than the four beats.

TURNING

Turning quickly is very important if you are racing. It is estimated that a good quick turn gains anything from a fifth to three-fifths of a second on a slow one at each turn, which will count considerably the farther the swimmer goes.

To turn quickly, the first thing to attempt is the approach to the side of the bath. This must be timed so as to reach it with the turning arm stretched out in front. You can do this by taking one long stroke or two or three short ones as you near the side of the bath. When your hand touches the bath side, just above the waterline, place the palm of the hand flat on it, the fingers pointing in the direction the body is going to turn, and level with the surface of the water. Then swing your body round, legs bent well at the knees, until the soles of your feet come into contact with the wall, a few inches below the surface.

Bring the hands rapidly to the hip, palms and fingers pointing frontwards and downwards, and then give a backward stroke, which brings the body right up against the side with the hips almost touching it. Then the arms are put forward, the legs are straightened out suddenly with a snap, and the body is allowed to travel on the impetus of the push off until it slows down, when the arms take a stroke. The legs do not move until the arms are recovering, when they fall into their proper action.

Many swimmers take advantage of the turn to get a deep breath. When they do so they put their head up above the surface of the water, instead of underneath, as in the ordinary style of turn.

POINTS TO REMEMBER

The four things most essential to an expert swimmer are : confidence, concentration, patience, and perseverance. Confidence in yourself to believe that what others have done you can do ; concentration on the task in hand ; patience to surmount all the difficulties that you will meet, and perseverance to attain the ideal and ambition you set before you.

It is not advisable to enter the water after a hearty

meal, or when exhausted after vigorous exercise. The best time is about two hours after a meal, when it will be principally digested.

Leave the water if you find it brings about a feeling of chilliness and a numbing of the hands and feet.

Leave swimming alone if you suffer from giddiness, faintness, palpitation, or similar affections. Ask your doctor's advice.

If you suffer from earache or deafness, do not enter the water without first plugging the ears with cotton-wool containing a little vaseline or other grease. In any case, it is advisable to plug the ears if you find the water an annoyance.

Keep cool. Never be flurried in action or breathing.

If you should accidentally fall in the water while you are fully dressed, remember that the air in your clothes will help to buoy you up for some time. Therefore, do not lose your head.

On learning to swim, bear in mind that the body is lighter than water and try to avoid any artificial aid, such as rubber rafts and water wings.

BOATING—AND THE RIVER

WHAT could be more pleasant, on a really hot summer afternoon, than to row up the river and tie up under some shady tree to while away the hours with a book or watch the little fish darting in the shallows?

If you cannot row you should learn to do so as soon as you can, so that the delights of the river are no longer denied you. A word of warning, however!—never, *never* take out a boat unless you can swim.

As a matter of fact, to be really correct, rowing is done with *oars*, one only of which is used by one person. Whereas, in *sculling*, one person operates a pair of sculls, which are somewhat shorter and lighter than oars. However, the action is very much the same.

It is impossible to row or scull effectively unless your feet are adequately supported by a stretcher, which in river boats should be a board leaning away from the rower or sculler at the top. The stretcher should be so adjusted that the legs are not quite straight out.

A boat should not be propelled by your arms, which ought to act merely as links between shoulder and sculls during the greater part of the stroke. Only towards the end of it ought they to be flexed, to bring the handles up to the body. Many people waste their strength by rowing entirely with their arms, which will stand any amount of work as mere connections, but in muscular power cannot compare with the loins and back, which make most of the effort in rowing.

To make a boat travel well and easily, the stroke

FIG. 1.

Good position at end of stroke: back straight: hands brought in to chest; eyes "in the boat."

should be as long as is consistent with applying power advantageously. The body should be brought well forward to begin the stroke and go well past the vertical to finish it. Also, the beginning of the stroke should be smart, so that the blade of the oar or scull grips the water at once. The pull must be as even as possible throughout the stroke, and the blade must be raised clear of the water smartly at the end by dropping the hands quickly, to prevent drag. (See Fig. 1.)

FEATHERING

Since the blade is large enough to offer considerable resistance to the air when moved quickly through it—especially against an adverse wind—the oar or scull should be "feathered" after the hands have been

FIG. 2.

The hand before (left) and after (right) feathering the oar.

lowered preparatory to bringing it forward, by dropping the wrists and revolving the scull through a quarter circle, till the blade is parallel to the water. Fig. 2 shows the position of the hands before (left) and after (right) feathering. If done too soon, before the blade is clear of the water, feathering may result in a "crab" being caught !

STEERING

If you want to go to the right (looking ahead from the bows) pull on the right-hand scull, and vice versa. If you are steering while someone else sculls, apply the rudder between strokes. Pull the rudder to the right if the boat is to bear left, and to the left if you wish to bear right.

SOME GENERAL HINTS

Do not watch your oar or sculls ; keep your eyes " in the boat " except when you glance over your

229

shoulder to steer clear of an obstacle. If a collision is imminent, jerk the handle of your oar upwards clear of the rowlocks, and push it towards the side of the boat. This allows it to swing back against the outside, blade towards the stern.

When hiring a boat make sure that the oars or sculls are properly paired and in good condition, and that the

Fig. 3.

(a) *Rowlocks will not be lost if attached to the boat by short pieces of cord.*
(b) *Oars shipped with blades towards the bows will not wet the seats or be damaged: and are more easily got out again.*

rowlocks are well greased. When shipping sculls always place the blades towards the bows if you have passengers aboard, otherwise water will drip over the seats.

Be careful on entering or leaving a boat; get some one to hold it, if possible. Never change seats in mid-stream—always draw in to the bank.

When travelling upstream, give a descending boat the centre and keep to one side; in descending, keep to the centre, except when meeting steamers, which have right of way.

SAILING

After a time, if funds permit, you may feel inclined to invest in a sailing-boat.

A good selection for a beginner is a centreboard dinghy, ten feet long by about four feet beam, with plenty of freeboard. The centreboard, by increasing the side surface, enables the boat to sail across the wind without being driven sideways, and make it more stable. A non-centreboard boat's sailing qualities may be much improved by fitting *lee boards* such as are used by Dutch boats and Thames barges. These are shaped as shown in Fig. 4, and hung over the sides of the boat ; that one being let down which is on the leeward side when sailing across the wind. The boards are suspended by short ropes, and each has another rope for hauling it up. A board is flat on the inside, but on the outside tapers off from the centre line to the edges. If the boat is round-sided, longitudinal pieces must be nailed on below the waterline for the boards to bed against.

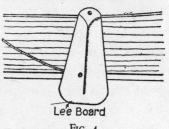

Lee Board

Fig. 4.

A lee board on a sailing boat.

All ironwork in the dinghy should be galvanized ; and ballast should fit the spaces in the bottom of the boat so that it may not shift—and be made secure. Airtight casings under the seats add considerably to buoyancy in case of swamping.

Expert advice should be obtained when a second-hand boat is being selected, as the number of possible defects is many. A freshly painted second-hand boat for sale should be regarded with suspicion.

SAIL AREA

The product of the boat's beam multiplied by its length gives roughly the number of square feet that a beginner's craft may carry with safety under all but exceptional conditions. As experience is gained the spread may be increased, but safety must come first.

BALANCING SAILS

A boat will not sail well across the wind or into it unless her sails are well balanced—that is, have the same area or leverage both fore and aft of the point in which the side resistance may be considered to be concentrated. Too much sail forward will make the boat try to turn her head away from the wind, unless the rudder is put over to windward ; while too much sail aft will make her try to turn into the wind, and require the rudder to be kept over to leeward. In either case there is a serious drag and loss of speed ; whereas a boat with well-balanced sails will almost run herself, and will make steering very easy.

In practice a boat should have a trifle too much sail aft, so that, if struck by a squall, she will naturally come up into the wind. A boat that falls away will be improved by reducing the jib or increasing the mainsail ; while too much sail aft is corrected by a larger jib or a smaller mainsail. The sailing balance can also be adjusted to a certain extent by shifting the ballast in the direction of the excess of sail.

HANDLING A BOAT

Fig. 5 illustrates various common nautical terms. The direction of the wind in each case is shown by an arrow, and the position of the boom by a heavy straight line.

"Luffing" means putting the tiller to leeward (rudder to windward) to bring the bow round into the wind. As this immediately relieves the pressure on the sails, it *must be done* if a squall strikes the boat when sailing close-hauled or square to the wind. If the wind is on the quarter (*i.e.* obliquely behind), slack the mainsheet or lower the sail instead of luffing, which would only bring the boat side-on to the squall and make things worse.

"Going about" signifies changing from one tack to the other. Before the operation begins the boat should be turned out of the wind a bit to give her plenty of way for the manœuvre. The helm is then put over to leeward smartly to make the boat swing round head to wind, until the boom moves over to the other side. If there are any passengers they should keep well down during the manœuvre, to avoid being hit by the boom. If the boat has too little way on her, or the operation is bungled, she may come up into the wind and stick there with her sails flapping idly. She is then "in irons." To get her going, put the rudder hard over in the direction to which she ought to turn, or push the jib out on the other side.

Gybing, or Jibing, which means a sudden shifting over of the boom when the wind is astern, may happen accidentally while running if the wind is not kept

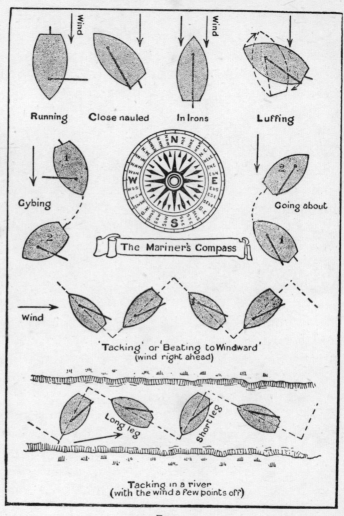

FIG. 5

Explaining various common nautical terms.

slightly on the side opposite to the boom. It is a dangerous occurrence when unintentional, as a great strain is put upon the mainsheet, and the boom may

knock passengers overboard. Should gybing be un-
avoidable, haul in the mainsheet until the wind
changes side, and then pay it out, being careful to
avoid letting the boat fall away sufficiently to provoke
another gybe.

RULES OF THE ROAD

It is essential that the nautical rules of the road
should be understood and observed to prevent col-

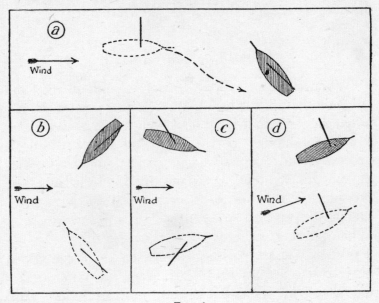

FIG. 6

*These diagrams illustrate sailing rules of the road.   The shaded boat
has right of way.*

lisions. A few of the most important are illustrated
in Fig. 6. In each case the boat which has right of way
is shaded.

(*a*) A boat running before the wind must keep

out of the way of a boat sailing close-hauled. (*b*) A boat sailing close-hauled on the port tack (*i.e.* with wind on the port side) must give way to a boat sailing on the starboard tack. (*c*) A boat running with wind on port side must give way to one running with wind on starboard side. (*d*) If two boats are running with the wind on the same side, the one to windward must keep out of the way of that to leeward. A fifth rule (not illustrated) is that boats travelling in opposite directions pass one another on the port side.

REMEMBER THESE HINTS !

When alone in a boat do not attempt to row and sail it at the same time. When sailing a boat do not fasten the sheet, but keep it in your hand, passed round a cleat or under a thwart to relieve the pull, if necessary, and ready to let go in a moment. Do not sit on the weather gunwale to counterbalance the pressure on the sail ; a sudden lull or heavy roll might throw you overboard. Keep on the seat. When steering, sit to windward of the tiller.

When you are passing to leeward of a large vessel, be ready to let go the sheet when the wind strikes the sails again. Give big ships in motion a wide berth, if possible, as the wash may be dangerous. A heavy wash should be met bows on.

If you venture on the sea with your sailing dinghy, avoid shallow water in which large waves are breaking. Do not run before a heavy sea, unless you have a drogue (sea-anchor), or the boat may broach-to and be swamped. A bucket tied to a float, or a bundle

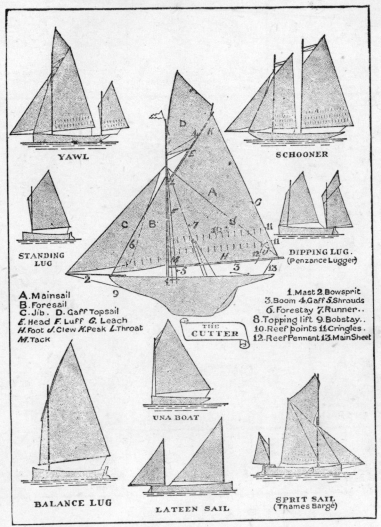

YAWL

SCHOONER

STANDING LUG

DIPPING LUG.
(Penzance Lugger)

A. Mainsail
B. Foresail
C. Jib.   D. Gaff Topsail
E. Head F. Luff G. Leach
H. Foot J. Clew K. Peak L. Throat
M. Tack

1. Mast 2. Bowsprit
3. Boom 4. Gaff 5. Shrouds
6. Forestay 7. Runner..
8. Topping lift 9. Bobstay..
10. Reef points 11. Cringles.
12. Reef Pennant 13. MainSheet

THE CUTTER

UNA BOAT

BALANCE LUG

LATEEN SAIL

SPRIT SAIL
(Thames Barge)

Fig. 7

Different kinds of rigs and (in centre) naming parts of sails, ropes, etc.

of oars, will serve as a makeshift drogue for a small
boat. If a rough sea gets up and you have a good

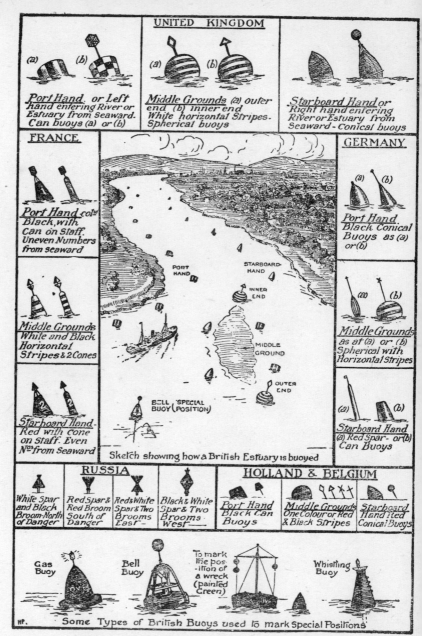

FIG. 8—BUOYS USED BY VARIOUS NATIONS.

drogue, the best thing is to lie-to on it. Be careful not to run aground at high water of spring tides, or it may be a long time before the boat gets off again.

A burgee (small triangular flag) flown at the masthead is useful to show the exact direction of the wind. When anchoring in a current, do not drop anchor until the boat begins to get stern way on her; and then pay out the chain gradually, so that it shall not foul the flukes.

When lowering a sail in a strong wind, gather it in quickly as it comes down, lest the wind should render it uncontrollable. Furled sails, unless they are tarred, should not be left exposed to the weather. But sails should never be covered up while damp, or more harm than good will result; nor should sails, even if housed dry, be left furled for a long time, or they will mildew.

Capsize a rope (turn it loose end downward) when coiled, so that the running part may be free. Carry a good baler and a lifebelt or two when passengers are aboard. Keep all blocks well oiled.

BUOYING OF CHANNELS

Fig. 8 shows the types of buoys used by various nations. In British waters port-hand buoys are flat-topped, starboard-hand buoys conical and one-coloured. On picking up a starboard buoy, steer to the left of it; and to the right of a port buoy. A middle-ground buoy, used for marking ends of shallows between two channels, is usually striped.

AT THE SEASIDE

THERE are so many exhilarating things to do at the seaside, such as having donkey rides and playing on the beach, that one is apt to forget the hundreds of tiny creatures and plants that live *in* the beach and the shallow pools ! They live there all the year round, long after the last holiday-maker has bought his stick of rock and gone home, so, if you happen to be near the sea in the winter, put on a warm coat and go down to the beach to see what you can find !

SHINGLE DWELLERS

The shingle beach and the tall cliffs look somewhat desolate in January, but look closely and you will find signs of life.

One of the most abundant animals at all seasons is the common Limpet. One limpet is not so much like another as at first appears : the shells vary enormously. A limpet shell presents the ideal form for withstanding rough water, and if you wear one down upon a grindstone the section so obtained will be almost exactly that of the most up-to-date sea walls. The more exposed limpets are low and rugged, but those farther out at sea, and so less exposed to the surf, make much larger and finer shells. A limpet can do with very little sea water ; just a few hours' immersion daily will keep it alive. By noting the distribution of the limpets you can get a rough idea as to the limit of high tide, and whether the coast is generally exposed to or sheltered from rough weather. Thus in Devon and Cornwall it often happens that limpets are more abundant on rocks facing north or north-west than those exposed to the full force of the south-westerly Channel gales.

By marking limpet shells and the piece of rock to which they are attached, their wanderings can be tracked, and it will usually be found that they go in search of food mostly when covered by water, returning to roost in the same place when the tide turns.

WINKLES

Almost as obstinate as the limpet in clinging to the rocks during stormy weather is the little Rough Winkle, of which you will find thousands on any coast. Having a round shell it cannot stand up to the waves in the manner of a limpet. It climbs just above high-tide limit, where the spray can still moisten its gills and keep alive the vegetable growths on which it feeds. It looks very like the common winkle, but is smaller, with a coarse-ribbed shell. Some scientists have sug-

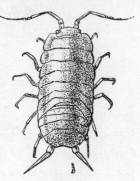

Fig. i.
Sea Woodlouse.

gested that it may be a near relative of the common periwinkle which, in the course of ages, is gradually changing from a purely aquatic life to one on land. A very interesting feature is the way in which it has changed its nesting habits to suit altered circumstances. Whereas the common winkle lays its eggs on rocks or weeds, the rough winkle keeps its young inside its shell until they hatch. This is perhaps one reason why it is never eaten, for the "family" makes the parent unpleasantly gritty to bite upon !

Quite as common on many coasts are the little Chink Shells. They look like very rough winkles, but if one of each is put in a glass of sea water it will

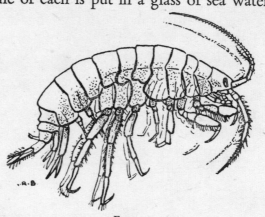

FIG. 2.
Sand Hopper.

be evident that the snail inhabiting the chink shell has two long streamers on each side of the horny cap (often miscalled a " head ") which is used to close the shell. As the name suggests, the chink shells hide in cracks and crannies from the force of the waves.

Even the bare-looking rocks, therefore, harbour plenty of life, and so too does the shingle. Under the loose stones you will find the big Sea Woodlouse and myriads of Sand Hoppers, or beach fleas as they are called (Figs. 1 and 2) ; and even in cold weather the rotting seaweed may be swarming with the maggots of various beach flies. Rotting weed soon becomes very hot, and the many creatures infesting it are all busy scavengers, doing useful work and having interesting life histories.

SEAWEED

High winds off the sea, when combined with the great underwater movements known as ground swells, invariably result in the beach being piled high with seaweed and all kinds of animals that in the ordinary

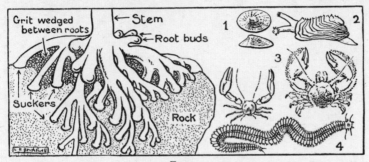

FIG. 3.

*The roots of a big "Cowtail Seaweed," and some of the "flat dwellers":
1, Chinaman's Hat Limpet; 2, Rock Venus Clam; 3, Hairy Porcelain Crab
and Long-horned Porcelain Crab; 4, "Cat" Worm.*

way live far out in deep water, and are beyond one's reach unless a dredge or trawl-net is used.

The Great Tangle, or Oar Weed, grows to twelve of more feet long, and the immense roots often harbour quite a little zoo. Seaweeds gather their nourishment straight from the sea water, and so do not require roots like those of land plants, which rely largely upon the soil. Look at the sucker-tipped "roots" of oar weed, and you will see that before the waves tore it

from the rock the spaces between the branching roots
became clogged with sand and grit, which was
gradually pressed into a compact mass. The smaller
a sea animal, the more enemies it has, as a rule, to hide
from ; and the roots of the weeds offer safe lodging
for a host of creatures. Fig. 3 shows just a few of these
" flat dwellers," but you will discover many more,

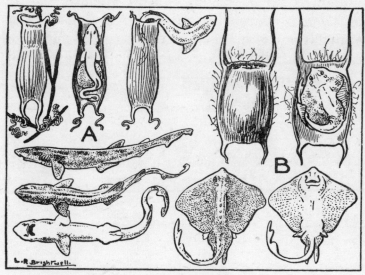

FIG. 4.
Egg cases and young of (A) *Dogfish, and* (B) *Skate.*

besides all kinds of animals, eggs, and other seaweeds,
on the leaves and stems of the tangle weed itself.

Among the banks of driftweed you will also find
skate and dog-fish egg cases (see Fig. 4), starfish, and
sponges—a mass of plants and animals. The barest
looking stones and bits of dead shell may bear signs
of life, for they are often fitted with innumerable
little holes, the work of the boring sponge, which eats

its way even into live oyster shells, causing the death of the occupants before they can be brought to market.

IN THE SPRING

With the first warm days of March the seashore becomes a very different place. Soon the shingle will hide many sea bird's eggs, often so cunningly marked as to be indistinguishable from the stones. But, even if your eyes are sharp enough to detect them, leave them in peace, and turn your attention to the sands and rocks.

To appreciate properly the wealth of life that now

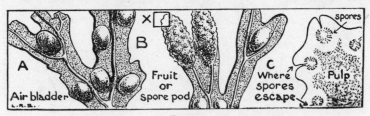

FIG. 5.

A, *Bladder Weed*. B, *Bladders filled with spores, or seeds*. C, *The piece marked* X *cut open and strongly magnified*.

begins to appear, you must take into consideration the sea water. A pocket lens or good school microscope, both of which are quite cheap, will be helpful.

The great majority of sea animals begin life as eggs, which may be laid upon the weeds or stones or cast adrift upon the waters. But, wherever they first appear, the animals which hatch from them make their way to the sea surface. There they live for varying lengths of time until old and big enough to return to the sea floor, or perhaps safely hold their own as grown-up animals in the open waters.

Just as on land all animal life is directly or indirectly dependent upon vegetables, so in the sea the plants are vital to the wellbeing of all other creatures. In the spring you will notice that much of the Bladder Weed (Fig. 5) bears heavy pimply bladders filled, not with air, but with a thick slimy substance. These jelly-filled bladders are the seed pods, and in time each gives up numerous little spores which float away into the water. Some may eventually settle down and grow into big seaweeds, others drift about among

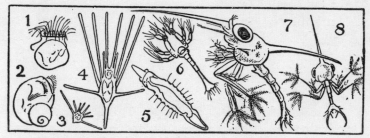

FIG. 6.

Sea Babies, much magnified : 1, Clam ; 2, Sea Snail ; 3, Starfish ;
4, Sea Urchin ; 5, Worm ; 6, Prawn ; 7 and 8, Crabs.

millions of even more minute plants that never change their form. All these scraps of life go to feed such creatures in their baby stages as are shown in Fig. 6, and these in turn may prey upon each other, or themselves be eaten by bigger beasts.

This medley of life is collectively known as Plankton, the Greek for " wanderers " ; and while many Plankton animals remain unnamed to this day, others are known to be the young of our common food fishes and shellfish.

Sea water gathers heat much more slowly than

does the air, but every day now the weather improves, and the sun's rays glancing off the sloping sides of the waves make the waves serve as forcing frames to the plants. What with this and such abundance of food, all animal life increases rapidly. The inshore water, too, is calmer now, and a host of creatures are making for the shallows to lay their eggs out of reach of the hungry foes that remain in the deeps beyond low-tide limit.

SUMMER-TIME

Among the fishes you will easily recognize in the summer are the Common Blenny and the Goby.

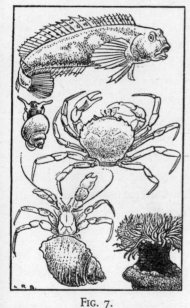

FIG. 7.

Blenny, Winkle, Shore Crab, Hermit Crab, Beadlet Anemone—all good in a sea aquarium.

FIG. 8.

Swimming Crab, Opelet Anemone, Limpet—all of these are to be avoided.

The latter lives mostly on sand stretches at low-tide level, but both fishes attach their beady eggs in firm compact masses to the undersides of stones. These eggs will hatch out in a basin of sea water, if it can be kept aerated with a syringe or by some other means. Each little fish, upon hatching, will be seen to have a big yolk sac attached to his underneath. On this sac they skate about in a lively manner until the yolk is absorbed. They will then require minute plant and animal food, and it will be kindest to set them free.

IN THE ROCK POOLS

Though a great many sea animals can be kept and watched to advantage in a glass tank or pie-dish for a day or two, there is for the amateur no aquarium like the natural rock or sand pool. Unfortunately, the wind often ruffles the water enough to hinder observation. This difficulty can be overcome by cementing a sheet of glass into the bottom of a bucket or biscuit tin, first cutting out the tin floor. "Water glasses" of this kind are used by naturalists all over the world, as well as by fishermen for collecting sponges, spearing shellfish, etc. Such a simple apparatus will open up a world of wonder which would otherwise be quite beyond one's sight.

Both rocks and sand swarm with life, though the rocks perhaps are the richer hunting grounds, since they offer more hiding places for the sea animals, and most of them are forced to spend much time in hiding, their world being so full of enemies. Conspicuous in every pool in the summer are the sea

anemones. The Beadlet and Opelet and the big
Dahlia are the common kinds, especially the first two.
Anemones are very simple animals, little more than
a big stomach attached to a circular mouth fringed
with numerous feelers or tentacles. These are hollow,
like the fingers of a glove, but inflated with sea water
instead of air. When the water is withdrawn the

FIG. 9.

A Dahlia Anemone capturing a prawn, digesting it, rejecting the odds and ends.

whole animal contracts into a mere blob of coloured
jelly.

The tentacles contain innumerable microscopic
darts which can be shot into anything they touch. If
this is some small animal it is at once paralysed. The
muscular stomach then engulfs it whole, digests all
the eatable portions, and rejects the waste by simply
turning the stomach lining inside out (see Fig. 9).
Sea anemones can be kept for weeks in an ordinary
pie-dish, especially if you are near the shore and fresh

sea water can be obtained. Little comes amiss to the sea anemone, and some will engulf animals almost as big as themselves.

NOW FOR THE CRABS

At very low spring tides you will often find the hermit crab crawling about in some borrowed shell. Fixed to the shell will very likely be a big Striped Sea Anemone (Fig. 10) that is always found in

FIG. 10.

A Hermit Crab with two Anemone lodgers. To the right is another, house-hunting.

partnership with the crab and nowhere else. This queer pair get on very well together, for each benefits from the other's society. The anemone can throw out bunches of stinging threads like masses of white cotton, and so makes a very unpleasant mouthful for any fish that might otherwise swallow the hermit, shell and all.

The anemone in its turn is saved the trouble of hunting, for it is always dinner-time with the hermit crab, and his flowerlike protector gathers the scraps that fall from his table. Often the hermit's house carries acorn barnacles—such as cover every rock and harbour pile. In addition, he may have the com-

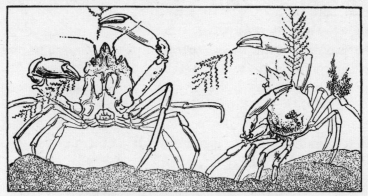

FIG. 11.

The Spider Crab goes in for fancy dress.

panionship of a very handsome white and chocolate coloured worm. It is about five inches long, and usually hides in the topmost spirals of the shell, which are not occupied by the soft tail portion of the crab. When a meal is in progress, the worm comes down to dinner, as it were, calmly helping itself to food and taking pieces from between the crab's jaws without that short-tempered householder showing any resentment.

Some very different types of crab come inshore in spring, and conceal themselves by dressing up. Their bumpy pear-shaped shells and long spindle legs might be easily mistaken for bits of rock and weed stems, but the crab is taking no chances, and deliberately plants all kinds of oddments about his grotesque body. These Spider Crabs, as they are called (Fig. 11), are of many kinds, and each kind has its favourite fancy dress. Some prefer bits of sponge, and others weed, while a few laboriously pile stones upon their backs.

A mysterious feature of the weed-costume crabs is that, although their brains must be almost negligible, they seem to know at once whether their dress harmonizes with their surroundings. An interesting experiment is to take a crab dressed in red weeds, place him in a basin of sea water containing only green weeds, and give him a night to himself to recover his nerves and "make up" in peace; for he dresses best under cover of darkness. By morning he will almost certainly have taken off all the red weeds and substituted green.

The reverse experiment works equally well, while a crab deliberately stripped of his costume will soon reclothe himself, if provided with material. The end of each scrap of weed selected is first chewed, to give it foothold, and then planted among the stiff-hooked hairs covering the crab's back and limbs. Since weeds so planted soon begin to grow, a decorated crab may in time look less like a living animal than a walking bush or animated forest.

AMONG THE ROCKS

Deep crannies between rocks are often literal mines of interest. In searching them an electric torch is useful, and it is as well not to thrust in your naked hand. A big crab or even a conger eel may be at home, and even if it does not take direct hold of a finger or two, it may so wedge the hand between itself and the rock as to make withdrawal impossible.

Very common at low tide are the curious creatures known as Sea Urchins (Fig. 12). At first sight an

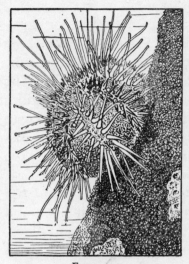

FIG. 12.

A Sea Urchin climbing a rock.

FIG. 13.

A magnified picture of his various spears, suckers, and pincers.

urchin appears to be a mere ball of shell, covered with spines, and showing no signs of life at all. Actually it is a near relative of the starfish.

Picture a starfish with the arms all bent round till the tips meet, and any spaces between filled in with plates of shell covered with spines, and you will have a good idea of how a sea urchin is constructed. Like the starfish it has innumerable suckers, or *tube feet*, as they are called, which can be pushed out at will through tiny holes in the shell. Place a sea urchin in water, and you will soon see these feet appear between the spines. Their round sucker tips take firm hold of the rock, one after the other, and haul the animal over the surface at rather more than a snail's pace.

FIG. 14.
Sea Cucumber.

A powerful lens or low-power microscope will show other organs beside the tube feet and spines (Fig. 13). The shell is covered with various kinds of pincers which snap up scraps of food and pass them to the mouth, in the middle of the urchin's under surface. If a dead sea urchin is cut open, it will be found that it contains a most complicated arrangement of hard stony teeth. This is really a kind of gizzard or grinding mill, and is known as Aristotle's lantern, on account of its appearance and the Greek philosopher and naturalist who first discovered it.

Among the same rocks will be found the Sea Cucumber (Fig. 14), another relative of the starfish. Though so unlike in general appearance, it has the same tube-like feet, and feeds itself very daintily, putting tiny scraps of food, invisible to the naked eye, into its mouth by means of five pairs of ragged fingered " hands."

EXPLORING THE SANDS

Warm weather and calm seas soon make the sands quite as populous as the rocks. Here again the animals tend to simulate their surroundings, for everywhere the business of eating and being eaten goes on apace. Sand work calls for rather different methods of collecting from those used on the rocks, where the ordinary spoon-net was useful but most of the work depended on sharp eyes and nimble hands. Most of the creatures living on the sand or in the water above it tend to burrow at the least hint of danger, and some are so cautious that they live permanently hidden, keeping in touch with the water by various ingenious devices.

At low tide, when the sands are left bare and dry, you can detect the presence of these burrowers only by means of various tell-tale marks upon the surface. Commonest of all land animals is the Lug-worm, used so largely as bait for line fishing. This worm lives very much as does our common garden worm, lying buried in the sands, which it continuously passes through its body, retaining what nourishment there may be in the way of microscopic plants and other eatables. The lug-worm always leaves two distinct marks to show that it is " at home " : first a round, basin-like hollow, and second, a few inches away, a familiar mound of castings (Fig. 15).

The Common Cockle makes a similar hole, but no castings, while the Masked Crab raises a little mound, from which only the tips of his feelers protrude. A spade soon brings these and many other beasts to light. They are all worth keeping in a glass jar of sand and sea water, where their various methods of burrowing can be watched at leisure. The masked crab keeps in touch with the life-giving sea water by bringing his feelers close together, so that the double row of stiff hairs on each combine to form a four-sided tube. The crab's various mouth parts serve as a pump and keep a constant stream of water flowing

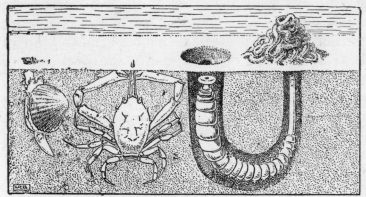

FIG. 15.
Cockle, Masked Crab, and Lug-Worm.

down the tube, to bring the necessary oxygen to the crab's gills.

Cockles, like all other two-shelled burrowing molluscs, manage in a rather different manner. They have two siphon pipes, one continually pumping water in, the other forcing it out. These two pipes may be enclosed in a leather case, as in the Gaper Clam (Fig. 16) or, like those of the cockle, they may be separate, though short and stout. All these clams and cockles bury themselves by means of a muscular foot, which in the case of the razor clam can often win a match against the most vigorously handled spade. By alternately swelling and contracting, this foot causes the shell to sink into the sand like a warm knife into butter.

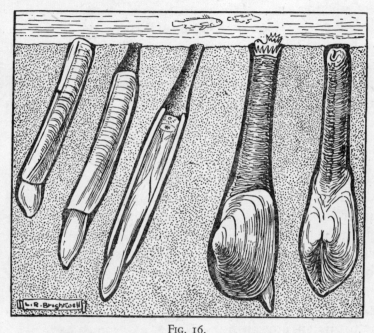

FIG. 16.

Three stages of the Razor Clam's boring. Next, the Gaper Clam with its long siphon.

The cockle can only bury itself just below the sand surface, for its foot is much smaller. But, to make up for this, it is vigorous enough to move its owner about the surface at a surprising rate. A few cockles in a basin of sea water will prove themselves to be as active as so many grasshoppers.

All our native clams and cockles are quite good to

eat, if gathered far away from any drain outlets. The common mussel pumps nine gallons of water through its system every twelve hours, and if a little colouring matter, or even dust, is placed in the water, the action of the siphon pipes will be at once apparent.

Sticking out of the sand in such numbers that at low tide they look like some kind of maritime stubble, you will find worm tubes of many kinds. If dug out very carefully and placed in sea water they reveal the living occupants, with peacock-tinted gills and long restless feelers. The latter are used to gather food, or to add layer upon layer of minute bricks to the sea worm's edifice.

All these animals desire to burrow deep into the sand, but there are many others equally anxious to do exactly the opposite. To avoid sinking, an animal must be mounted on legs like a prawn's, or else be flattened like a Sand Star or Sole. The flat fish, gobies, and many other sand dwellers bury themselves partially by fluffing up the sand around their edges. A number of sea creatures also have the wonderful power of taking on the same colour as their surroundings, and it forms an interesting series of experiments to place various sand fish, crabs, etc., in a small aquarium, such as a pie-dish, with different coloured and patterned floors. Some patterns will be much more readily imitated than others, and the rate at which new colours can be assumed varies according to the animal's species, age, and state of health.

A champion " chameleon " of the sea is the little Sand Cuttle, a near relative of the octopus, which is exceedingly abundant on most sandy shores. Sometimes you may find it trapped in tidal pools, but in sunny weather this and many other sand dwellers can be taken in shallow waters with an ordinary shrimp net, which may easily be made at home. The cuttle-fish, though a mollusc, is provided like the true fishes with myriads of pigment cells ; and as certain of these are closed down or opened up, so the colour varies. The cuttle can swim backwards by puffing water vigorously through its siphon pipe, which is also used to eject a cloud of ink if its owner is alarmed. When shrimping you may see dozens of these tiny ink clouds bursting and forming miniature screens, under cover of which the cuttle-fish make good their escape.

Perhaps the most fascinating of all hunting grounds is a Zostera bed. These great banks of emerald sea grass occur all round our coasts, and not only the grass but also the sand about its fibrous roots always swarms with life. Under the eaves of the roofs formed by the overhanging grass blades, you may take a dozen kinds of fishes in a single scoop of the shrimp net. Most tend to imitate the colours of the grass, but the common Pipe Fish (Fig. 17) and his several relatives carry this still further and even imitate the grass blades in general shape. In summer you will often find the pipe fish with a sack of eggs attached to his waistcoat portion. Indeed the sack is formed of two flaps very much like the big waistcoats fashionable many years ago. These protect the little pipe fishes until they hatch. In the pipe fish tribe, as with a good many shore fishes, it is always the father fish who takes upon himself the care of the family.

The quaint slug-like creature called the Sea Hare

is a great frequenter of Zostera beds. Though somewhat formidable in appearance it is perfectly harmless.

FIG. 17.

*A sea meadow. Attached to the weed are, top, shells and Bell Anemones.
The swimmers include a Wrasse, Pipe Fish, Stickleback, and Crab ; and on
the shingle is a Sea Hare.*

When alarmed it puts up a " smoke screen," not of
sepia, like the cuttle's, but of a lovely violet colour,
which can be used to dye a handkerchief, though in
time the colour fades to a rusty brown.

WHEN AUTUMN COMES

At the approach of chilly October, most sea animals retreat into deeper water. There they are well beyond the raging surf, and the temperature fluctuates less than between the limits of high and low tide. But still in the shelter of the sea wall, or by the harbour piles, you may find animals that can defy

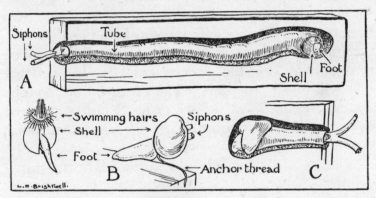

FIG. 18.

The Ship Worm : A, *in a block of wood ;* B, *the young worm alighting ;*
C, *beginning the burrow.*

the winter's gales even more successfully than the hardy limpet.

Some of them are destructive pests, particularly to timber. Often the winter gales will cast upon the beach big baulks of timber riddled with winding burrows over a foot long by half an inch wide and neatly lined with shell. These are the work of the Ship Worm (Fig. 18), which in the old days of our "wooden walls" helped to sink more ships than did ever storm or cannonade.

Actually, it is not a worm at all, but a relation of the cockle, wonderfully modified for its peculiar way of life. The fragile tube, if very carefully separated with a saw or chisel from the wood, will be found to present at one end two tiny clam-shaped shells, between which lives a shellfish with a short foot and two long siphon tubes extending to the full length of the tube. The foot is used to give the clam a leverage, whereby it rocks its shells and slowly but surely drives a tunnel through even seasoned oak. Some boring clams will even tunnel through a fellow shellfish, but a ship worm meeting such an obstacle turns aside, a habit which is responsible for the various bends and turns that you will find in its tubes. The open end of the tube ensures free access to the sea water, which is pumped in and out of the siphons as by the cockle and other clams.

One would think old oak sufficiently hard for a delicate clam shell to destroy, but the Common Piddock (Fig. 19), though no stronger of shell, even tunnels limestone. The chalk at Black Rock, Brighton, and the much harder limestone at Swanage, in Dorset, are fairly honeycombed with these and other similar clams. Like the ship worm, they do their work of destruction by keeping up a rocking motion. Their tunnels are not so long, however, but only just adequate to enclose entirely the animal's two shells.

A tiny crustacean called the Gribble (Fig. 20), a cousin of the woodlouse, or pill bug, so common in our gardens, does enormous damage to timber, eating into it just as the caterpillar of the death watch beetle spoils old furniture. When numerous, as they usually are, they are capable of making massive timber look like so much sponge.

One of the most common of all creatures upon the harbour piles is the Acorn Barnacle, which some people mistake for a small limpet with the top rubbed off. The open top is really closed by four shutters, but in a dish of sea water the barnacle will thrust

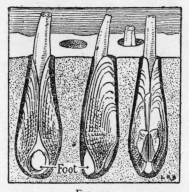

FIG. 19.

Piddock Clams in stone.

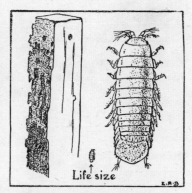

FIG. 20.

The Gribble and his work.

these aside like tiny folding doors, and put out the six pairs of feathery limbs with which it combs the sea water for any chance eatables present. The barnacle develops from a tiny free-swimming creature that swarms in the open sea during summer months. Later it settles down, grows hard tiny shells round its body, and spends the rest of its life eating.

L. R. B.

INDEX

The titles of chapters are given in small capitals. Figures in italics denote solutions to puzzles.

PRINTED IN GREAT BRITAIN AT
THE PRESS OF THE PUBLISHERS